THE LAYMAN'S BIBLE COMMENTARY

THE LAYMAN'S BIBLE COMMENTARY
IN TWENTY-FIVE VOLUMES

THE LAYMAN'S BIBLE COMMENTARY

Balmer H. Kelly, *Editor*

Donald G. Miller   *Associate Editors*   Arnold B. Rhodes

Dwight M. Chalmers, *Editor, John Knox Press*

VOLUME 6

THE BOOK OF

JUDGES

THE BOOK OF

RUTH

THE FIRST AND SECOND BOOKS OF

SAMUEL

Eric C. Rust

JOHN KNOX PRESS

ATLANTA, GEORGIA

10 9 8 7 6 5 4 3 2

Complete set: ISBN: 0-8042-3086-2
This volume: 0-8042-3066-8
Library of Congress Card Number: 59-10454
First paperback edition 1982
Printed in the United States of America
John Knox Press
Atlanta, Georgia 30365

PREFACE

The LAYMAN'S BIBLE COMMENTARY is based on the conviction that the Bible has the Word of good news for the whole world. The Bible is not the property of a special group. It is not even the property and concern of the Church alone. It is given to the Church for its own life but also to bring God's offer of life to all mankind —wherever there are ears to hear and hearts to respond.

It is this point of view which binds the separate parts of the LAYMAN'S BIBLE COMMENTARY into a unity. There are many volumes and many writers, coming from varied backgrounds, as is the case with the Bible itself. But also as with the Bible there is a unity of purpose and of faith. The purpose is to clarify the situations and language of the Bible that it may be more and more fully understood. The faith is that in the Bible there is essentially one Word, one message of salvation, one gospel.

The LAYMAN'S BIBLE COMMENTARY is designed to be a concise non-technical guide for the layman in personal study of his own Bible. Therefore, no biblical text is printed along with the comment upon it. This commentary will have done its work precisely to the degree in which it moves its readers to take up the Bible for themselves.

The writers have used the Revised Standard Version of the Bible as their basic text. Occasionally they have differed from this translation. Where this is the case they have given their reasons. In the main, no attempt has been made either to justify the wording of the Revised Standard Version or to compare it with other translations.

The objective in this commentary is to provide the most helpful explanation of fundamental matters in simple, up-to-date terms. Exhaustive treatment of subjects has not been undertaken.

In our age knowledge of the Bible is perilously low. At the same time there are signs that many people are longing for help in getting such knowledge. Knowledge of and about the Bible is, of course, not enough. The grace of God and the work of the Holy Spirit are essential to the renewal of life through the Scriptures. It is in the happy confidence that the great hunger for the Word is a sign of God's grace already operating within men, and that the Spirit works most wonderfully where the Word is familiarly known, that this commentary has been written and published.

THE EDITORS AND
THE PUBLISHERS

THE BOOK OF

JUDGES

INTRODUCTION

This book and the Books of Joshua, First and Second Samuel, and First and Second Kings make up a section in the Hebrew Bible termed the "Former Prophets." Modern scholarship associates these books with the Book of Deuteronomy and ascribes them to what is generally known as the Deuteronomic school of historians. This school of writers seems to have flourished towards the end of the pre-exilic period and during the Exile, that is, in the seventh and sixth centuries B.C. It was characterized by the moral outlook of the great prophetic figures from Amos, Hosea, and Isaiah onwards, which had also shaped the final form of the Book of Deuteronomy, and it took many of its leading motifs from the latter book. These historians viewed history as the scene of moral retribution. They were convinced of the divine judgment on sin and, like the great canonical prophets, believed that it was worked out in history both at the national and at the individual level. If Israel sinned, its punishment was sure, and deliverance could come only through repentance. So also with individuals; they, too, could not expect to escape the consequences of their wrongdoing. Because of their prophetic affinities, these historians also showed an interest in the prophetic figures who appear in Israel's history, and emphasized the place of the Spirit of the Lord and of "charismatic" or Spirit-possessed personalities in Israel's early history.

The Historical Situation

The Book of Judges deals with the period of Israel's history which followed the conquest of Palestine, when the people were settling down in Canaan. Two major issues faced the Israelites. The first was a social and national issue. It was concerned, in part, with the relations of the Israelites to the original inhabitants, the Canaanites. It seems clear that here there was no policy of wholesale extermination, but rather there were slow assimilation and intermarriage, commingled with some war and extermination. The first chapter of Judges discloses this slow process and makes it clear that pockets of Canaanites remained in Israel long after the Conquest. For example, the Jebusites at Jerusalem were not subdued until David's time. Yet open conflict seems to have been rare after the initial period of conquest, and only in the story of Barak and Sisera (Judges 4 and 5) do we find an account of war between the Israelites and the Canaanites. Much more significant at the social level were the foreign invasions. In these early days of unrest, when the land was changing masters and internal friction was present, surrounding nations like Edom, Moab, Ammon, and the nomads of the desert all sought to profit by the state of affairs. Invasions were frequent, and many of these are recorded in the Book of Judges.

Side by side with the social and national issue was the religious one. The Israelites, coming in from the desert, had brought with them a monotheistic and imageless worship and a high moral level, as the Decalogue reveals. Their life had been that of desert nomads, mainly pastoral in character, not directly dependent on the fertility of the soil and little concerned with the agricultural festivals associated with seedtime and harvest. The Canaanites, on the other hand, were an agricultural people, whose religion was bound up with sustaining the fertility of the soil and with the cycle of nature. They had many deities, as archaeology reveals, and these deities show few moral characteristics. They included male gods and female consorts whose sexual relations kept the cycle of the seasons in motion. Associated with their worship were sexual orgies which were believed to influence the gods by sympathetic magic and so produce fertility of soil and plentitude of crops. This type of religion is called a "fertility cult." In Canaan it was celebrated at high places or holy places on the hilltops. Sacrifices were offered here on the altars, and priests sought to obtain guidance from the deities by practicing oracular divination. Here were the stone pillar or "mazzebah" and the wooden stock or "asherah," possibly a remnant of a sacred tree. The names of the principal Canaanite deities were Baal, the male god, and Astarte, his female consort. Astarte was similar to Ishtar, the Babylonian goddess of love and fecundity, and the figure of a female goddess of this type was familiar throughout the ancient Near East. When the Israelites settled in Canaan and began to follow agricultural pursuits, it was natural for them to fall away from the desert ways of strict morality and "puritanic" principles into the loose and licentious worship of the Canaanite Baalism, associated as it was with the agricultural life of the community. Only in time of war and disaster would the mass of Israelites tend to remember God, the God of war who had delivered them from Egypt, brought them through the wilderness, and led them into Canaan, giving them victorious passage and conquest. In easier times they fell into the fertility worship and practices of their neighbors.

These two issues appear throughout the Book of Judges, and in the central section, from 2:6 to 16:31, they are linked together by the Deuteronomic editors of the book by means of the doctrine of divine retribution. In this part of Judges we find a repetitive pattern in the recorded history. Israel sins by going awhoring after the Baals (local manifestations of the chief "Baal"), and forsaking the Lord; God sends judgment in the form of invasion by some marauding host; Israel repents and cries to God; God raises up a "judge" or "savior." Thus the process is one of sin, judgment, repentance, and deliverance.

Literary Structure and Theological Treatment in the Central Section

We shall look at this central section of the book (2:6—16:31) first, since it constitutes the most important part. The editors were undoubtedly dealing with very much earlier material, some of it contemporary with the events with which it is concerned. This material may have been preserved down through time, partly in oral and partly in written form, although it was probably all committed to writing in the early days of the monarchy, and there seems evidence for a shorter and pre-Deuteronomic edition of the Book of Judges. What the Deuteronomic editors did was to take this material, in whatever form it came to them, and put it into their framework of sin, judgment, repentance, and deliverance. This is not to imply that such elements were not present in the original situation, but rather that the editors drew them out and emphasized them for their purpose of teaching the prophetic lessons of history. If God reveals himself through history, then history must disclose his presence in judgment and in mercy. The Deuteronomic history writers recognized this, and thus sought to write the history of Israel in the light of God's presence, underlining the lessons it taught and drawing out into the open the often hidden forces of human sin and divine judgment which lay in the deeps of historic events.

The Deuteronomists did, however, introduce a certain degree of artificiality into their history, by endeavoring to fit a series of detached and often local incidents into a more continuous and nation-wide scheme. This framework consists of an introductory formula, recounting Israel's sin, God's judgment in the shape of invasion, Israel's repentance, and God's sending a "judge" or "deliverer," and also of a closing formula which recounts the years of peace that followed under the judgeship of the hero concerned. The periods of oppression and judgeship are apparently artificial, consisting usually of multiples or fractions of forty years. Examples of those summaries are 3:7-9 and 3:11, in the story of Othniel; 3:12-15 and 3:30, in the story of Ehud; 4:1-3 and 5:31c, in the story of Barak and Deborah; 6:1-2, 6-10, and 8:28, in the story of Gideon; 10:6-16 and 12:7, in the story of Jephthah; 13:1 and 16:31, in the story of Samson. The deliverers and the incidents connected with them are also far more local than national. Only in the case of the campaign of Deborah and Barak against Sisera do we seem to have a national action in which all the tribes participate. Apart from this, the stories are mostly concerned with one of the following groups: the tribe of Judah, the people occupying the hill country of Ephraim, the groups on the border of the Philistine coastal strip, the Israelites across Jordan, and the Hebrews around Shechem. Although the Deuteronomic formula suggests all Israel, the stories seem to indicate that the judgeships were much more local. We note that the word "judge" here is best and primarily rendered "deliverer" or "savior," since these heroes were primarily concerned with delivering the people from foreign oppression. Quite evidently, however, once they had established their position by military prowess, they assumed also the other and, for us, more normal function of judgeship, that of administering justice and governing the community.

There were six major judges—Othniel, Ehud, Deborah and Barak, Gideon, Jephthah, and Samson. To these the Deuteronomic editors added six more names—Shamgar (3:31), Tola (10:1-2), Jair (10:3-5), Ibzan (12:8-10), Elon (12:11-12), and Abdon (12:13-15). Concerning these minor judges very little of historical value is offered, and they seem to have played no significant role in the forward movement of the history of God's people. It is difficult to understand why they were included, unless the editors were anxious to round off the number of judges at twelve.

The Introductory Section

The central section of Judges is preceded by an introductory section (1:1—2:5), which is really a continuation of the story of the conquest in the Book of Joshua, and makes it evident that the conquest of Canaan was a slower and less thorough job than the Book of Joshua would lead us to suppose. This embodies some early and very valuable historical material.

The Appendix

The last five chapters of the Book of Judges constitute an appendix in which is preserved some valuable historical material (chs. 17-21). We have the story of the migration of the tribe of Dan from its original place of settlement in the center of Palestine to its final location in the north around Laish, together with the way in which it founded and furnished its famous sanctuary at Dan (chs. 17-18). We have also the story of the outrage at Gibeah and the tragedy that befell Benjamin (chs. 19-21). This preserves some valuable evidence about Israelite custom and practice and about the sacking of Jabesh-gilead; it also includes some folklore, like the story of the maidens of Shiloh, which has a historical core and may indicate a marriage ceremony.

The Chronology of Judges

The Deuteronomic pattern raises the question of the chronology of Judges. If we allow for the wilderness wanderings, the period of conquest, the judgeship of Samuel, and the reigns of Saul and David, we are left with a period shorter than the total chronology of Judges requires. If we allow that the judges were local rather than national figures, they may have overlapped. Furthermore, the artificial appearance of the periods of oppression and judgeship seems to indicate that we must not place too much reliance on the chronology of Judges itself. We may say that the events recorded go back to the twelfth and eleventh centuries B.C. and that some may be even earlier if there were Hebrew groups in Palestine prior to the main invasion of the Josephite tribes across Jordan, which seems to be supported by archaeological evidence.

The Sources Behind Judges

The sources from which the Book of Judges was built were, we have suggested, written and oral traditions. Sometimes there seem to have been two traditions of the same incidents. Thus chapter 4 recounts the story of Deborah and Barak in prose and is paralleled in chapter 5 by a poetic account, which by its form and content seems much more realistic and early. Chapter 5 is generally regarded as contemporary with the campaign against Sisera. It clearly regards Sisera as the leader of the Canaanite forces and a king in his own right, whereas in the prose version of chapter 4 the leader is Jabin, and Sisera is only his general. It may be that two campaigns are involved—one of Zebulun and Naphtali against Jabin of Hazor and one by Deborah and Barak against Sisera—and that chapter 4 has sought to combine them. We shall see that the Gideon story contains two versions which have been skillfully woven into the single account of the Deuteronomists. There may originally have been two invasions. Gideon has two names, the other being Jerubbaal. He kills two pairs of kings of the Midianites—Oreb and Zeeb (7:24—8:3) and Zebah and Zalmunna (8:4-21).

We need to remember that we are dealing in this book with the dawn of Israelite history. This was mainly preserved in oral form during the early period, and thus it raises real historical questions. But what matters is its theological significance, what God was seeking to teach Israel through these events, of whose details we cannot be altogether certain, and what word of God they have for us in our day and time.

OUTLINE

The Invasion of Canaan and the Settlement. Judges 1:1—2:5

Israel Under the Judges. Judges 2:6—16:31

The New Generation—Apostasy and Judgment (2:6—3:6)
Othniel (3:7-11)
Ehud and the Moabites (3:12-30)
Shamgar and the Oxgoad (3:31)
Deborah and Barak (4:1—5:31)
Gideon and Abimelech (6:1—9:57)
The Minor Judges—Tola and Jair (10:1-5)
Jephthah the Gileadite (10:6—12:7)
The Minor Judges—Ibzan, Elon, and Abdon (12:8-15)
Samson and the Philistines (13:1—16:31)

Appendix: The Story of Dan and the War
with Benjamin. Judges 17:1—21:25

The Migration of Dan and the Story of Its Sanctuary (17:1—18:31)
The War with Benjamin (19:1—21:25)

COMMENTARY

THE INVASION OF CANAAN
AND THE SETTLEMENT

Judges 1:1—2:5

This opening section of the Book of Judges provides a summary of the period of the conquest of Canaan. The divine oracle was consulted to discover the order in which the tribes should take the land. The indication, presumably by the method of sacred lot, was that Judah and Simeon should start the campaign.

The whole chapter reads like a parallel to the account in Joshua. If the latter represents more the point of view of the northern tribes, this chapter gives us an account of the Conquest from the standpoint of the southern, especially that of the tribe of Judah. It would appear that the account covers the period of conquest that begins in the Joshua record in Joshua 10. The Israelites, encamped at Gilgal, are there described as moving out in several tribal movements to possess the land. In the Judges account, which we are now considering, Joshua is not mentioned, and the editor, to provide some connection with the preceding Book of Joshua, provides the opening formula which stipulates that all this happens after Joshua's death. If Joshua were the hero of the northern tribes, we can understand the reticence about him in a tradition emanating from the south.

Judah and Simeon proceeded southwestward and engaged Adoni-bezek. The road of invasion led to Jerusalem, and we are told that on the way they captured Adoni-bezek and treated him as he had once treated seventy captive kings. They apparently left him mutilated, and his followers brought him to Jerusalem where he died. There follows an account of the siege and sack of Jerusalem by the Judahites. This would seem to be in conflict with the repeated statements elsewhere that the Jebusites held that city in the midst of Israel until David's time (Joshua 15:63; II Sam. 5:6-10). Adoni-bezek is probably to be identified with Adoni-zedek, the king of Jerusalem, whom Joshua fought according to the tradition preserved in Joshua 10:1-5. The Joshua account mentions the sack of other cities but not that of Jerusalem, thereby conforming to the references just given. There is,

however, nothing to militate against a capture of Jerusalem
which was earlier than David's campaign and only temporary,
from which the Jebusites recovered, managing to retain their in-
dependence.

Having subdued Jerusalem, the Judahites fought the Canaanites
in the hill country south of Jerusalem, in the lowland or Shephelah to the west and southwest, and in the Negeb, the southern
area bordering on the desert. They secured Hebron. This city was
inhabited by the Anakites, as its former name, Kiriath-arba,
indicates, since Arba was the father of Anak (Joshua 15:13).
The military leaders who were defeated, Sheshai, Ahiman, and
Talmai, are described in Joshua 15:14 as descendants of Anak
(compare Numbers 13:30-33, which describes them as giants).
Joshua 15:13-19 provides an interesting parallel to the verses
now under consideration. It attributes the defeat of these heroes
and the capture of the city to Caleb, whose Kenizzite tribe was
a constituent element of Judah (see Num. 32:12; 34:19). Caleb
is mentioned in the Judges account in connection with Debir.
Having captured Hebron, the victorious Judahites advanced on
Debir, which was captured by the brother or nephew of Caleb,
Othniel, who by his prowess thus secured the hand of Achsah,
Caleb's daughter, who had been promised by her father to whoever conquered the city. Caleb also gave a source of water supply at the request of Achsah. The account here does not give
sufficient details for identification of the site. Debir was to the
southwest of Hebron, on the edge of the Negeb, and water supply was a problem on the fringe of the desert belt.

In verses 16-21 our attention is directed to a Kenite group,
bound up with Moses by his marriage (see Exod. 2:21) and
another constituent element of the tribe of Judah. They went
from Jericho, the city of palms (cf. Judges 3:13; Deut. 34:3),
and settled near Arad, south of Hebron. Hormah was also secured. The hill country was possessed, but the Canaanites retained the fertile valleys, aided by their military strength and
chariots of iron. The Israelites are thus seen as moving down
from the hills into the valleys and slowly infiltrating the land,
the very picture given by archaeology. We are reminded in verse
21 that Jerusalem remained in the hands of the Jebusites.

The interest now turns from the Judahites to the Josephite
tribes of Ephraim and Manasseh. We are told that the house of
Joseph went up from Gilgal (implied) to secure the important

center of Bethel. They secured the city by a strategy, subverting one of the inhabitants. The account shows that pockets of Canaanites remained in this area, sometimes in fortified cities. The cities mentioned indicate that the Israelites were confined here to the central hill country, being cut off from the fertile Plain of Esdraelon to the north by the Canaanites of Megiddo, Taanach, Ibleam, and Beth-shean, and from the area occupied by the Judahites by the Canaanites in Gezer. Once more we have the picture of infiltration from the hill country to the valleys and a slow taking over of the land.

The tribes of the north were in similar strait; Zebulun, Naphtali, and Asher dwelt in the midst of the Canaanites, slowly subduing them. The tribe of Dan never established its position and the Book of Judges later records its migration (Judges 17-18). Aijalon was in the hill country northwest of Jerusalem. Thus Dan was originally in the center of Palestine, even though its final settlement was in the north. The section that refers to Dan (vss. 34-36) is the only one in this chapter that has the term "Amorites" instead of the usual "Canaanites."

In 2:1-5 we are told of the transfer of the religious center from Gilgal to Bochim, once the invasion was to some degree accomplished. We shall have occasion later to discuss the angel of the Lord. It suffices here to note that the phrase indicates the divine presence in a form perceptible to the senses. The word "angel" means "messenger." We have here a "theophany," a divine appearance in visible form. However the oracle came, the Covenant faithfulness of the Lord to Israel was reaffirmed. The Deuteronomic writers made much of the Covenant theme and also stressed God's promise of the land. Israel's disobedience in making a covenant with the Canaanites was now to be matched by the persistence of the Canaanites in their midst. Assimilation, not annihilation or armed expulsion, would now be the order of the day. The Canaanites would be adversaries whose very religion would be a perpetual temptation to the Israelites. In this way the Deuteronomic editors introduced their interpretation of the period of the judges. The place Bochim has not been identified. It may have been so called from the statement in 2:4 that the people wept on hearing God's message.

ISRAEL UNDER THE JUDGES
Judges 2:6—16:31

The New Generation—Apostasy and Judgment (2:6—3:6)

We have in these verses a picture of the state of affairs that followed the Conquest. Actually verse 6 seems to connect with Joshua 24:28, where we likewise read that Joshua dismissed every man to his inheritance. Thus 1:1—2:6 seems to be an insertion that breaks up the continuity. Joshua's burial is described and the details of Joshua 24:29-31 are repeated; Timnath-heres is evidently another name for Timnath-serah (Joshua 24:30). After Joshua's generation—that is, his contemporaries—died off, a new generation arose which became enamored of the agricultural gods of Canaan, the Baals and the Ashtaroth, and did not know the Lord, who had brought Israel from Egypt. The implication is that the new generation did not know God by firsthand encounter in historical events, and thus found it easier to fall into apostasy.

We have already discussed this situation in the Introduction and shall not repeat it here. The Canaanite deities Baal and Astarte are given in their plural form, a reminder that every locality had its own peculiar form of the deities. Since the process of settlement was one of absorbing rather than exterminating the inhabitants, and since the way of life was increasingly agricultural, we can understand that the Israelites in any locality would tend to fall into the religious practices of their neighbors and forget the God of their wilderness experience. At least a generation away from their great deliverance, and with pressing agricultural rather than pastoral needs, they turned to deities who were supposed to protect and extend fertility.

The editor of Judges proceeds to outline the scheme we have already discussed in the Introduction—apostasy, judgment, repentance, and deliverance in successive cycles. Native oppressors and foreign invaders plundered Israel. We note that the divine judgment of Israel is not in some catastrophic intervention but rather through the normal processes of history—oppression and invasion. This is characteristic of the prophetic view of history and judgment, whereas later apocalyptic thought (represented in the Old Testament fully by Daniel and also in anticipation by

Joel, Ezekiel 38-39, Zechariah 9-14, Isaiah 24-27) emphasized
catastrophic intervention of a supernatural variety and heightened
the effects in the description of such judgment in order to under-
line its supernatural aspect. Israel's repentance under the judgment is a reminder that in Old Testament thought the divine
wrath has an evangelizing motif. Judgment is God's work to make
men realize their sin and moral bankruptcy and so turn back to
him. God's forgiveness was given historical expression in the
appearance of the judges or deliverers, endowed with special gifts
of prowess and military skill because the Spirit of the Lord
rested on them. We note that these deliverers or saviors can be
described as saving Israel. This is a reminder that, in the early
days, salvation was thought of in physical and material terms.
It was a part of the divine education of Israel that the nation
had to be led through the outward to the inward, and to learn
that salvation ultimately means deliverance from the inward
bondage of sin and not merely deliverance from the outward
tyranny of military oppressors.

Judges gives a picture of Israel's repeated infidelity. The nation
persists in transgressing the Covenant. Here the reference is to
the relation which God established with his people on Sinai. We
shall discuss the idea of "covenant" as a mutual bond between
persons later, when we come to the story of David and Jonathan.
It was a significant aspect of Israel's faith that the relation among
men could, under the guidance of revelation, be used as an
image to express God's relation to the nation. Such an image
debarred any idea of a relation of natural descent whereby God
was ancestor of Israel. He was under no natural necessity to care
for them. The bond between him and his people was a moral
bond. At the human level, two parties entered into a covenant by
the mutual imposition and acceptance of obligations, but at the
divine level, it is God who initiates the Covenant and who de-
cides the terms by which it must be regulated. He chooses Israel
and demands moral obedience, laying upon the nation the moral
obligations of the Decalogue. On his part, he promises to be
faithful to his Covenant, and Israel, in accepting, does likewise.
Hence, to break the Covenant by failing to fulfill its obligations
and obey God's will is equivalent to treachery. It is transgression
of the Covenant, and God will not allow such defection to go
unpunished. Persistent defection must lead to a state of affairs
in which Israel is continually reminded of its sin. Hence, the

continuance of the Canaanites in the midst of Israel and of the foreign nations in its borders was held to be a test of Israel's faith. In judgment and in mercy, God was confronting Israel with his Covenant demands.

The closing verses of this section (3:1-6) list the nations with whom Israel dwelt in contention. The five "lords" of the Philistines were the five "tyrants" who, in the Aegean style, ruled in the five city centers of the southern Philistine coastal area. The "Hivites" is a reference to the Hurrians who penetrated like the Hittites (also mentioned) down into this area and left behind pockets of settlers. The "Sidonians" were the Phoenicians in the northern coastal area. The "Jebusites" survived as a separate people into David's time. The ultimate fate of these peoples is indicated in verse 6.

Othniel (3:7-11)

Israel followed after the Baals and the Asheroth. The last term is the plural of "Asherah," the name of the female consort of "Baal," the chief Canaanite god. It is also used in the singular of the wooden pillar which symbolized the goddess at the local shrines. Thus we have here an indication of the lapse of the Hebrew peoples into the loose and licentious paganism of the Canaanite inhabitants. The change from the pastoral ways of the wilderness wandering to the agricultural practices of settled life in Palestine tended to turn their eyes from the God of Sinai to the fertility gods and goddesses whom their Canaanite neighbors regarded as guardians of the soil. Such defection from the religion given to Moses brought down the judgment of God. The Deuteronomic editor sees this in the invasion of an Aramean group led by a king, Cushan-rishathaim, who has not been identified with any leader mentioned in archaeological sources. The reference defies more accurate definition. Israel repented, however, and God raised up a "judge." The better rendering of this word is "deliverer" or "savior," one who has the power to deliver the people from their oppression. The man raised up, Othniel, was a nephew of Caleb and thus a member of the Kenizzite clan in the tribe of Judah. Evidently the issue was more local than national, and the invading force may have been a Midianite tribe, for the Midianites were on the fringe of Judah.

Othniel is described as a charismatic person, one upon whom

the Spirit of the Lord had come. The word for "spirit" in Hebrew can also mean "wind." In the early days the Spirit of the Lord was regarded as a windlike force that could invade a man's personality and be responsible for extraordinary activity on his part. This activity might vary from brute strength, as in the case of Samson, through skill in war and leadership, as in the case of Gideon, through craftsman's wisdom, as in the case of Bezalel (Exod. 31:2-5), to moral and spiritual insight, as in the case of the prophets. All were alike gifts of God, and often the windlike nature of the Spirit was manifested in the early days in the abnormal and ecstatic behavior of those who were possessed by the Spirit, as in the case of Saul.

Using his customary formula for the first time, the Deuteronomic editor now declares that the land enjoyed security for forty years.

Ehud and the Moabites (3:12-30)

The Oppression by Eglon (3:12-14)

Once more (vs. 12a) Israel did evil in the Lord's sight, and the judgment descended. As we have noted, there is no indication that the judgeships recounted in this book were either over or on behalf of all Israel or that they were chronologically successive. The editor has gathered a series of detached and often local incidents into a history of the whole people. The locale of this new oppression was not Judah but Ephraim. The invaders penetrated as far as Jericho, the city of palms. The oppressors were Moabites, allied with Ammonites and Amalekites, who were desert Bedouins, and led by Eglon, the Moabite king.

Ehud and Eglon (3:15-25)

The cycle of penitence was repeated. Israel cried to the Lord and he raised up another deliverer. This time it was a Benjaminite, Ehud. Benjamin bordered on Ephraim, and was probably invaded too, so that one of its tribesmen became the champion of the hill country of Ephraim. Ehud undertook to take the tribute money to Eglon, and secretly prepared a short double-edged sword which he concealed under his clothes and girded to his right thigh. He secured admission to the king and presented the tribute. Then, on the pretext of having a secret message for

Eglon, he managed to secure a private audience from which all the royal attendants were excluded. This audience took place in the king's roof chamber, a cool single room erected on the roof of the palace. As the king rose to receive the message, Ehud smote him in the belly with the hidden dagger. The Hebrew realism appears in the description of Eglon as a fat man into whose fat the dagger sank beyond the hilt. The assassin withdrew with calm restraint, closing and locking the double doors of the roof chamber. The attendants assumed conditions to be normal, but at last they discovered the murdered Eglon. Meanwhile Ehud had been given sufficient time to escape.

The story is not an edifying one, but it is paralleled by other stories from this period. That Ehud should be described as a "savior" sent by the Lord may raise questions in our minds, but we need to remember the rough times in which this happened and must judge Ehud's treachery in this light. Still further, it would appear to be the divine strategy with Israel to educate men by enabling them to move from the physical to the spiritual levels. "Savior" here refers to salvation from oppression and thus to an outward thing; yet the people could learn through it, in the process of the centuries, the deeper lesson that the outward conditions result from the inward state of sin, a truth that the Deuteronomist editor is seeking to elaborate. Then true salvation must be from that inward state and not just from the outward conditions. In this sense the use of the word "savior" or "deliverer" can point beyond itself to God's final act in Jesus, while the association with God of even a crude act like that of Ehud at least emphasizes the truth that salvation is of God alone.

The Discomfiture of Moab (3:26-30)

Ehud, aided by the polite attitude of Eglon's attendants when they discovered the closed doors of the roof chamber, had made good his escape beyond "the sculptured stones" to Se-irah, an unknown location. He summoned Israel to his aid, and the people descended from the hill country of Ephraim. They secured the fords of Jordan so that the Moabite army of occupation, struck into a panic by the news of Eglon's death, was cut off and completely annihilated. Once more Israel had peace, and this is stated in the customary Deuteronomic formula with its repetitive time pattern.

Shamgar and the Oxgoad (3:31)

Shamgar is mentioned as one who delivered or judged Israel, but the customary formula is absent, and the foes are the Philistines, who do not appear until much later chronologically. Shamgar is probably a Hurrian name. The oxgoad was a long wooden pole provided with a metal tip at one end and a metal blade at the other, used to clean the plowshare. With this unusual but formidable weapon, he is said to have slain six hundred Philistines. There is something reminiscent of Samson about Shamgar. The two heroes are described as fighting the same foe, although the mention of Shamgar in the Song of Deborah (5:6) would imply that the foes were Canaanites rather than Philistines in Shamgar's case.

Deborah and Barak (4:1—5:31)

In these chapters we have two accounts of the last struggle between the Israelites and the inhabitants of Canaan itself, the Canaanites. The rest of the Book of Judges is concerned with foreign invaders, the Moabites, the Edomites, and the Ammonites from across the Jordan, and the Philistines from the coastal belt of the Mediterranean Sea.

Here the story of the oppression by the Canaanites under Jabin is given in two forms—a prose account in chapter 4 and a poetic description in the Song of Deborah in chapter 5. The song is generally agreed to be very early, probably contemporary with the events and giving an eyewitness account of them. The prose story is later, but it fills in some details lacking from the poetic description, although it also presents some problems.

The problems presented in these accounts have to be faced by any intelligent Bible student. According to Judges 4 the oppressor is Jabin, king of Canaan, who reigns in Hazor, and who may be identified with the Canaanite king of Hazor against whom Joshua fought, as recorded in Joshua 11. Sisera is the captain of Jabin's host and dwells in Harosheth-ha-goiim. In Judges 5, Jabin is not mentioned and Sisera is the oppressor, leader of a strong Canaanite federation, and himself of kingly status. Some contend that Judges 5, as a contemporary record, gives the true picture in which Canaanite opposition to the invading Israelites is led by

Sisera, king of Harosheth, and that the name of Jabin occurs in Judges 4 through the mixing of this story with the story of the subduing of Jabin already recorded in Joshua 11. On the other hand, Jabin as a Canaanite kinglet may well have been a member of the confederation, but whereas Judges 4 appears to elevate his position, Judges 5 does not mention him, making it clear that the real leader of the oppression was Sisera.

The scene of the oppression appears to have been in northern Canaan, centering in the fertile plain of Esdraelon. The invading Israelites had so far been confined to the hills, but this rich plain offered a great attraction for them, and its Canaanite cities made a last attempt to subdue them. In the plain there were fortified cities like Taanach and Megiddo. Moreover, Sisera was helped by the petty jealousies and disunity among the Israelite tribes themselves. As a consequence the Hebrew peoples were held back and oppressed for twenty years (4:3). We note that Sisera had a large mobile army of iron chariots, nine hundred in number (4:3), a reminder that the Iron Age had begun, and that the Israelites still had something to learn from the Canaanites about the new methods of warfare; they were joining issue with a highly efficient war machine.

The deliverance came at the hands of two remarkable people —Deborah, the prophetess, and Barak, the man of war. The charismatic nature of the judgeship is immediately evident in the case of Deborah, the prophetess. Her sex is a reminder that even in the early days, the Spirit of the Lord was not confined to the male sex. The prophets were essentially charismatic personalities on whom the Spirit of the Lord descended, and who, at this time, were often whipped into an ecstatic state in which they gave utterance to inspired words. As in the days of the early Christian Church, so also in early Israel, the presence of the Spirit of God in a man was associated with abnormal emotional and physical characteristics. On the other hand, the personalities of Moses and his successors, the great literary prophets from the eighth century B.C. onwards, are reminders that moral discernment and spiritual insight were still more fundamentally a sign that the Spirit of God was pervading a man's being. The behavior of Deborah indicates that these moral and spiritual qualities were present beneath the ecstatic and emotional overtones of her experience. Under her inspired command, Barak became the commander who led the Israelites to victory in battle.

The Prose Account: The Oppression of Jabin and the Leadership of Deborah (4:1-9)

The period of oppression came upon the Israelites because they did evil in the sight of the Lord. What this phrase covers seems to be indicated in 5:8—there was a religious defection on the part of Israel, who chose new gods. Believing in the living God who had delivered them from the hands of the Egyptians, covenanted with them on Sinai's height, fought their battles for them, and brought them into their promised heritage, they, a pastoral people, now found themselves in an agricultural community where a war leader and wilderness guide was not so important as a guarantor of the fertility of the soil. Such guarantors were ready to hand—Baal, the fertility god of the Canaanites, and Astarte, his queen consort. There was every temptation for the Israelites to desert the living God and adopt the beliefs and practices of the Canaanites among whom they dwelt, whose sexual fertility rites and pagan orgies formed a strange and yet seductive contrast to the rigid "puritanism" and strong moralism of the wilderness religion.

The judgment of God descended. We note that this judgment is worked out within the process of history itself. The Canaanites, bent on driving out this troublesome people who were stealing their land, turned on the invaders who had been attracted by their religion, and proceeded to oppress them. But they were instruments in God's hand, serving not their objective but God's. History moves under God's control.

So here, God raised a savior, a judge, and the judge was a woman, a reminder that women can exercise prophetic and creative leadership in God's plan. We note that Deborah seems to have exercised some of the functions of a judge in our modern sense. The people went to her for adjudication and advice. Actually this is of one piece with her prophetic function. Careful research has shown that the legal structure of the first five books of our Bible grew in a variety of ways around a Mosaic nucleus. There were, first of all, customs and rulings of past generations which came to have an authoritative status. Such laws were administered by the priests, who conserved the past and applied it to the present. At the same time, fresh precedents were continually being created by the elders who sat at the gate and sought to meet new situations, and by the prophets who in oracular consultations sought to give the mind and will of God on some specific issue. Deborah appears to have functioned in this case not only as a prophetess but also in a way akin to the elders dispensing justice at the gate. The reference to the palm of Deborah may be a confused memory of another Deborah, the nurse of Rebecca, who was buried under an oak in the same district of Mount Ephraim at Bethel (see Gen. 35:8).

The people came to Deborah to seek for oracular guidance from God. Through his prophetess the Lord commanded Barak to assemble an Israelite army at Mount Tabor, about twelve miles from Megiddo at the northeast of the Plain of Esdraelon. This was a strategic center for commencing a campaign. To meet the Israelites on this prominent hill, Sisera had to cross the plain and ford the Brook Kishon. This was a dried-up wadi in summertime, but with the winter rains it became a raging torrent (see 5:21). Deborah's prophecy appears to be particularly concerned with this latter issue, since the destruction of Sisera's army is associated with the brook, and the Song of Deborah records that the natural elements under God aided in the triumph (5:20-21). Deborah was persuaded to accompany the army, to encourage the leader and his men, and she prophesied that the ultimate triumph would not depend upon Barak but upon the feat of a woman. The sequel makes it clear that the reference is to Jael and not to Deborah herself.

We note that the only Israelites recorded as participating in the conflict are the men of Naphtali and Zebulun (vs. 6). The poem of chapter 5 adds several tribes to the list and is the more valuable source here.

The Prose Account: The Battle of Kishon (4:10-16)

Barak gathered an army of ten thousand men together at Kedesh, and Sisera assembled his chariots and warriors, summoning them from the extent of the Great Plain. The two armies came to battle at the foot of Mount Tabor. According to Josephus a storm helped in Sisera's defeat, and, as suggested above, this may certainly have caused the flood in the Brook Kishon mentioned in 5:21. This thesis seems to be supported by the declaration of Deborah that the stars in their courses, the forces of nature, fought against Sisera (5:20). Further, Deborah's own words, "Does not the LORD go out before you?" (4:14), might suggest a gathering storm, since the manifestations of the Lord

on Sinai, and in the Old Testament time generally, are often
associated with storm phenomena. In these scientific days such an
idea might be called in question. Yet the scientist no longer speaks
of deterministic causation, preferring rather to limit his task to
describing the regularities of nature and offering, as a scientist,
no attempted explanation of the deeps that may be present beneath the phenomena that he studies. As Christians we believe
that God is the Creator and Sustainer of the natural order. His
control over the forces of our world is something which the scientist as scientist can neither confirm nor deny. Such an affirmation belongs to the insight of faith. The atheist and naturalist
may deny it, but the man who believes that "what is seen was
made out of things which do not appear" (Heb. 11:3) is still free
to affirm it. It is a striking fact that in these early days, God was
thought of as a warrior God, coming to the assistance of his
people through the phenomena of nature. The Canaanite god,
Baal, was also a storm god and, in the thought of the contestants,
the struggle may have been a contending of the deities as well as
of the armed hosts. The triumph of the Lord through the storm
threw the Canaanites into dismay. In their rout, they were pursued, harried, and slaughtered by Barak, while their leader, Sisera,
fled on foot. This triumph confirmed Israel's wilderness faith and
demonstrated the might and power of the Covenant God who
had already manifested his love to his people.

We note the incidental reference to Heber the Kenite in
verse 11. The Kenites were a nomadic tribe closely akin to Israel,
and some were actually included as constituent members of the
tribe of Judah. Heber is mentioned because of the part played
subsequently by his wife Jael. The fact that he had separated
himself from his people is mentioned to explain how a Kenite,
who normally would live with his people at the southern boundary of Judah on the edge of the desert, was to be found in
northern Palestine.

The Prose Account: The Death of Sisera (4:17-24)

Sisera found refuge in the tent of Jael, the wife of Heber the
Kenite. Her seeming kindness reassured him. He turned aside
into her tent, partook of refreshment, and lay down to sleep
covered by her with a rug. Once asleep, Sisera became her victim
and died at her hands. The mode of his death is interesting,
since the instruments of it, a tent pin and a hammer, are remind-

ers that among the Bedouins it was woman's task to pitch the tent. The Bedouin hospitality beguiled Sisera into trustfulness; moreover, he was apparently ignorant of how closely the Kenite clan in general, and Heber in particular, had become bound in with Israel. Thus Deborah's prophetic prediction was fulfilled and victory was assured to Barak and his forces.

The ethics of this deed raises some real issues for the Christian conscience. Can good ever be accomplished by treachery and deceit? We have to remember the ruthlessness of the time, but it is noteworthy that not even the editor can describe this as a divinely inspired deed. It certainly stands condemned in the light of the Christian revelation. The fact that Deborah prophetically declared this outcome does not mean that the seal of God was on it. Let us say that Sisera's sin brought its own reward and that Jael's act was of one piece with that sinful involvement in which the Canaanite leader had been caught up. Jael's deceit and treachery became instruments of the divine justice as demonstrations of the truth that sin brings about its own destruction.

The Song of Deborah: The Praise of the Lord (5:1-5)

We turn here from prose to poetry. The story is much more vividly told than in the prose record. It carries all the marks of an eyewitness account, has a high degree of dramatic interest, and conveys a feeling of the very battle itself. The noise of the chariots of war, the wild war music, the thunder of the storm, and the rush of the flood resound through its verses. Further, the poetry demonstrates by its structure that the Hebrews had already, by the time it was written, attained a good understanding of psalmody. This song is the most characteristic example of early Hebrew poetry. We can see the structure quite clearly. Hebrew poetry was built upon the twin ideas of parallelism and rhythm. By parallelism is indicated the dual line structure of the poetry, in which the second line either repeats in another form or image the idea of the first line, or moves beyond the idea of the first line amplifying and extending it, or expresses the antithesis of the idea in the first line. Verses 19 and 20 give good examples of the first type:

> The kings came, they fought;
> > then fought the kings of Canaan,

. . . .

> From heaven fought the stars,
>> from their courses they fought against Sisera.

Sometimes this structure is built up in three lines rather than two, as for example in verse 7:

> The peasantry ceased in Israel, they ceased
>> until you arose, Deborah,
>> arose as a mother in Israel.

Rhythm means that the accent on the Hebrew words forms a structural pattern, which is repeated in the successive lines. We notice that the principle of rhyming, characteristic of Western poetry, is not found in Hebrew versification. The poem demonstrates its early nature by the presence in it of archaic forms and outmoded spellings.

The song opens with a sounding forth of praises to the Lord. He is pictured as dwelling on Mount Sinai, the place where he had shown himself to Moses and covenanted with his people. He comes from Seir and he marches through Edom, the Hebrew parallelism identifying the two, since Seir and Edom are names for the same region (see Gen. 32:3). The next verse declares that he comes from Sinai and that the mountains shake before him. Evidently the author of the song connects Sinai with Seir, a connection also found in another early poem, the Song of Moses:

> The LORD came from Sinai,
>> and dawned from Seir upon us (Deut. 33:2).

This would seem to place the holy mountain in Midian.

The thought that God's presence was localized in Sinai must not be taken to indicate a failure to grasp his universal nature, although it is true that at this early stage in the revelation the Hebrew had not grasped much that is meant in our technical term "omnipresence." Throughout the period of the Old Testament revelation there was retained, however, alongside the growing realization of God's all-pervading and universal presence, an emphasis on his special presence in specific places for the furthering of his purpose. His presence on Sinai's height was matched later by his presence in the Ark on the mercy seat between the cherubim, his special dwelling in the Holy of Holies in the Temple, his choice of Zion as his footstool, and his manifestation in the Temple through the presence of his glory or his "Shekinah." All this was a prefiguring of the Incarnation, for Christian faith believes both in the universal presence and immanence of God and in his special presence in the God-man, Christ Jesus, for us men and for our salvation. Furthermore, the special presence of God on Mount Sinai and in the Temple is matched by the special indwelling of his Spirit in the Church, which is the Body of Christ.

It may well be that in her own distinctive way and within the limitations of her thought, Deborah, if author she be, is endeavoring to convey the truth that the God who is fighting for his people is the God who showed himself specially and savingly to them in the manifestation on Sinai's height.

The passage is reminiscent of a later passage by a prophet in Isaiah 63:1-6 where God is pictured as coming to avenge and redeem his people as a mighty warrior from Edom, glorious in his apparel and traveling in the greatness of his strength. The whole presents a picture of God as a man of war whose purpose is the deliverance of the people whom he has chosen. This figure of war and conflict is one which repeats itself in the New Testament as well as in the Old. Our Lord is portrayed by Paul as doing battle with the powers of darkness, principalities, powers, the spiritual rulers of darkness in high places, in order to set free those who trust in him. In the Cross he made a show of these powers openly and triumphed over them (Col. 2:15). Their seeming triumph in the Crucifixion was turned into defeat on the Resurrection morning. The Book of Revelation has the picture of Christ as a victorious warrior who has descended from heaven, going forth to fight for and deliver his people (Rev. 19:11-16). Jesus himself sees his task as a conflict with the Devil and his demons, and as his disciples announce the success of their mission he triumphantly declares that already he sees Satan fall like lightning out of heaven (Luke 10:18). Christ's victory on the cross and in the empty tomb is almost impossible to express in cold, rational language, but it conveys the truth that he sets men free from sin and death by an act in which he triumphs over the demonic forces that hold men in thrall. No longer as God's people must we fight against Canaanites and earthly foes, but the story of the Old Testament prefigures the deeper conflict in which we wrestle with spiritual rulers of darkness in high places and in which we are delivered by the Word made flesh.

The Song of Deborah: The Pre-War Situation (5:6-8)

The song also portrays the apostasy of Israel and the disastrous results in lack of security. Farming and travel were alike impossible. Because the Israelites went after the gods of the Canaanites they lost their vision and their strength. The Canaanites dominated them so that they walked in fear. Verse 8 suggests that the Israelites were poorly armed. They had been deprived of weapons as well as of spiritual dynamic and the courage to resist. In such conditions God raised up Deborah. (For "Shamgar," see the comment on 3:31.)

The Song of Deborah: Praise and Reprimand (5:9-18)

The first three verses of this section are obscure in the Hebrew text. The chiefs and princes are summoned along with the travelers to rejoice at the way God has used the humble villagers of Israel to triumph over the prosperous Canaanites. The text suggests that the people are called to rehearse the triumphs of God to the accompaniment of music, the last part of verse 11 picturing Israel as it assembles in response to this call.

There follows a list of those tribes which participated and those which did not participate in the battle, praise and scorn respectively being accorded to them. Ephraim, Benjamin, Machir (the principal clan of Manasseh), Zebulun, Naphtali, and Issachar gave direct support. A glance at the map shows that these tribes cover the area of northern Canaan most affected by Sisera's domination. Reuben was as ever indecisive, a mood reflected also in the Joseph story (Gen. 49:4a). Gilead or Gad stayed across the Jordan, Asher remained by its seashore, and Dan refused aid. The latter reference speaks of the Danites abiding in their ships. Later in Judges (ch. 18), the story of the Danites is given in more detail. We shall see that, at some period, the tribe migrated from the central position to their final location in the north. They do not appear to have dwelt on the coast at any time, but in their northern location they may well have had contact with the Phoenicians, who were a seafaring people, and may have been employed as sailors. Asher was in the hills above the coastline, which was inhabited by the Phoenicians. It has been suggested that the reference indicates that some Asherites had found homes in the Phoenician cities of the coastal belt.

The Song of Deborah: The Battle Scene (5:19-22)

The battle has already been considered, but the added details in this song are significant. The location was Taanach, about four miles from Megiddo. It is implied that the Brook Kishon, which is called "the waters of Megiddo," was turned into a raging torrent resulting from a storm. The poetess sees this storm as a sign that God was using the elements of nature to fight for his people, a picture in keeping, as we have already noted, with the association of God's appearance with storm phenomena. The picture of God coming from Sinai across Seir and Edom may be an attempt to portray the advent of the storm sweeping up from the southland as a sign of God's presence with his people. God rode on the storm cloud as on a chariot (see Ezek. 1). There follows a portrayal of the army of Sisera in complete rout, punctuated by the beat of the fleeing horses. The confusion of battle, the raging storm-swollen torrent of Kishon, the chariots of war in desperate flight—all rise up before our eyes in these vivid verses.

The Song of Deborah: The Failure of Meroz and the Feat of Jael (5:23-27)

In verse 23, Meroz, a village in the line of Sisera's flight, is cursed for not apprehending him. The story of Jael is told in detail, and blessings are called down on her. We have already discussed the ethical problems raised by this story.

The Song of Deborah: The Palace of Sisera (5:28-31)

The song finishes with a dramatic portrayal of the mother of Sisera watching expectantly for the return of her son in triumph and showing impatience at his delay. Her ladies seek to comfort her by picturing the rich spoil that he is busy dividing and with which he will return laden. There is a kind of pitiless gloating here, as the song portrays the impatience of the mother, the comfort of the ladies of the court, the mixture of hope and fear which pervades the atmosphere of the palace, while all the time Sisera is dead. Evidently Sisera is no mere captain of hosts but a king in his own right.

We note the addition by the editor of the Book of Judges, recording that the land had peace for forty years.

Gideon and Abimelech (6:1—9:57)

The story in these chapters appears to be of a composite structure woven out of two traditions of the campaign of Gideon
against the Midianites. It has been suggested that 8:4-21 retains
one of these traditions, but it is generally agreed that it is almost
impossible to separate the strands. There are poetic elements in
the present text which seem to indicate that, like the song of
Deborah in the preceding chapter, the story of Gideon may have
had a long history in oral tradition and been given a poetic form.

In this epic we pass beyond the war with the inhabitants of
Canaan, to the protection of Israel's territorial gains and agricultural enrichment against the inroads made by the Bedouins of the
surrounding desert lands.

The Oppression of the Midianites (6:1-10)

The usual record of Israel's apostasy and defection is matched
this time by invasion from without, instead of by oppression from
within. God permitted invading nomads to lay waste the land to
such an extent that Israelites fled to mountain hide-outs and
strongholds. For seven years, as harvest drew near, these hordes
swept in and lived on the spoils. The text indicates that, as in all
such nomad invasions, the invaders brought their tents and families with them, camping in the midst of the agricultural wealth
that Israel should have garnered, driving away the Israelite peas-
antry, and spoiling the land like a swarm of locusts. Their work
accomplished, they returned to their desert fastness once more, to
await the next harvest season. Their use of camels marks a new
challenge to the Israelites. The latter had to deal with chariots of
iron when fighting the civilized inhabitants of Canaan, and now
they had to concern themselves with the swift-moving and organized camel raids of the Bedouins. There is little doubt that this new
phenomenon and its surprise tactics contributed to the discom-
fiture of the Hebrews.

We are told that the invaders were mainly Midianites, desert
peoples from the country lying south and east of Moab and Edom,
and actually blood kin to the Hebrews, as the story of the patriarchs reveals (Gen. 25:1-6). With them came Amalekites from
the southern desert region below Judah, and Bedouins from the
east across Jordan. Their depredations carried them as far across

Israel as Gaza in the area occupied by the Philistines, but the area around Shechem seems to have suffered most. Gideon, like most of the other judges, would appear to be a local rather than a national figure.

A prophet appears and God speaks through him to the people in response to their cry for deliverance. We note how all through these early records the emphasis falls upon the prophetic consciousness as a medium of the divine revelation. In this case, the words of the prophet recount the great deliverance from Egypt which God had already wrought and emphasize the divine command that people should not worship the gods of the land which they are to possess. Yet this latter injunction has been broken.

The Call of Gideon (6:11-24)

The story of the call falls into two parts, the account of Gideon's confrontation with a divine messenger by the winepress and the narrative of his breaking down the altar to Baal. These may constitute two distinct accounts of the call, but, if so, they have been so well combined that they are to be considered as two elements in the same story.

Gideon's father is described as Joash the Abiezrite and thus as a member of the tribe of Manasseh. Gideon was threshing wheat by the winepress when the angel of the Lord came and sat under his father's sacred oak. The word "angel" means literally "messenger." This angel assumed human form and, as in most of the early part of the Old Testament, signified a manifestation of God himself, a theophany. It is difficult to say whether the visitation was a vision or an actual man possessed of a prophetic consciousness, who could be regarded for the time of his message as a visible appearance and extension of the Lord. For Gideon, the angel was God himself in visible form. This is indicated by the statement in verse 14, that "the LORD" turned to him and spoke to him. The words of the angel of the Lord were the words of the Lord, and the encounter with the angel was an encounter with the Lord himself. The same understanding is found also in the story of the patriarchs (for example, Gen. 16:7-14). It is still true today that God can meet and arrest, challenge and comfort us, through other men and women whom we sometimes describe as being angels of God to us, messengers in and through whom the Lord has encountered us.

The declaration of the heavenly visitant, "The LORD is with you, you mighty man of valor," called forth from Gideon skeptical doubts as to whether God could be with a people who had suffered so sorely. He recounted God's mighty deeds of deliverance in former days at the Exodus from Egypt, and declared that Israel's subservience to the Midianites was a sign that God had forsaken his people. The reassurance of the angel that Gideon was chosen of God to deliver Israel served but to call forth protestations of inadequacy and weakness. Again the call was issued, and Gideon craved a sign which would confirm that God was showing him favor. He prepared an offering to the Lord and, directed by the angel, placed it on a rock. Its consumption by fire confirmed his call. The angel had vanished and Gideon, now convinced that he had encountered God's messenger, was struck with fear. He had been in intimate contact with God and that portended death (see Exod. 20:19; 33:20). We have here the recurrent experience of all who stand thus in God's presence. The consciousness of moral guilt, the sense of unworthiness, the feeling of inadequacy—we find them repeated again and again, as in the instances of the calls of Isaiah, Jeremiah, and Ezekiel (Isa. 6:5; Jer. 1:6; Ezek. 1:28—2:1). Only a feeling of utter inadequacy and moral insufficiency can fit men to be God's instruments. As the lips of Isaiah were touched by the glowing coals from the altar and as the Spirit of the Lord stood Ezekiel on his feet, so here the Lord spoke directly to Gideon and encouraged him: "Peace be to you; do not fear, you shall not die." Gideon perpetuated the words in an altar which he erected on the site of the encounter with God and which he named "The LORD is peace."

The Altar to Baal (6:25-32)

The second element in the call of Gideon is the destruction of the altar to Baal which his father possessed. This altar discloses that Joash, like most of his Israelite contemporaries, had succumbed to the paganism of his Canaanite environment and was participating in the worship of the Canaanite pantheon and in the fertility rites associated with it. The mention of the Asherah beside the altar is a reference to the wooden poles set up in Canaanite sanctuaries. They may have taken the place of sacred trees or they may have been conventional emblems for the ancient Semitic goddess Asherah. In any case they were part of the pagan rites. Acting by stealth and at night, Gideon followed divine instructions—destroyed the center of heathen worship, erected an altar to the Lord, and offered a bullock as a sacrifice. If Gideon received a call to deliver Israel from the Midianite oppression, some ask, why did he begin with a religious reformation in his own family? This need raise no problem. It is a prerequisite of God's victory over our foes that we must ourselves first be put right with him. Only when we are ourselves reconciled to him can we expect deliverance from the tyrants, spiritual or material, that oppress us. Our God performs his mighty works through regenerate people.

The men of the city awoke in the morning to find an accomplished fact. They demanded that Joash deliver up his son to death because of the sacrilegious act. Gideon's father took the position that this was a contest between the Lord and Baal, and that the gods must be left to fight it out. We are reminded of the later incident on Carmel's height when Elijah challenged Melkart, the Phoenician Baal, to a contest with the God of Israel. The issue was whether Baal was a god of power or just an empty and vain thing: Baal ought to be able to look after himself. The powerlessness of the pagan deity was manifested in the name that was now given to Gideon—"Jerubbaal," "Let Baal contend against him" (see 7:1). Gideon's survival after his destruction of Baal's altar would be an indictment of Baal himself.

The Sign of the Fleece (6:33-40)

Now the Midianites commenced their annual invasion, crossing the Jordan and encamping in the Valley of Jezreel, a broad valley that opens into the Jordan from the Plain of Esdraelon. The fertility of this area was a particular attraction to the marauding hosts.

We note the charismatic character of Gideon's leadership. A literal translation of the Hebrew of verse 34 is "The Spirit of the LORD put on Gideon." Through God's Spirit, Gideon became a kind of extension of God's personality. God's Spirit put on Gideon like a garment, and Gideon was possessed by a power from beyond himself. The description is unusual but is paralleled later in the New Testament. The experience of life in the Holy Spirit is so ineffable in the New Testament that its authors exhaust all possible ways of describing it. The Christian life is life in the Spirit, it is dwelling in Christ or in his Spirit, it is Christ or his Spirit dwelling in man, it is putting on Christ. The outpouring of

the Spirit on the whole Church foretold by Joel and declared an
accomplished fact by Peter on the Day of Pentecost (Joel 2:28-
32; Acts 2:16-24) is already prefigured in the lives of Old Testament saints, prophets, and heroes; and here, too, there is a like
variety of description.

Gideon, led by the Spirit, sounded the alarm and summoned
together his Israelite defenders. Manasseh, his own tribe, rose in
response and was joined by men of Zebulun, Naphtali, and Asher.
These other tribes may have entered the battle later, as 7:23 suggests.

The Israelite leader, however, still had his doubts. The sign
given through the acceptance by God of his offering either was
not sufficient or else is duplicated in another tradition by the story
of the fleece. In any case, God was put to the test. Probably it was
a second test. Gideon needed a reinforced faith to deal with the
marauding bands. The test may appear to us a very material one,
but we need to remember the rudeness of the times. So often in
these early days it was on the material level that God approached
men. They learned the reality of the deeper and spiritual levels of
life through the mediation of the physical and material. Often in
this period salvation was deliverance from material bondage and
oppression, yet it pointed to the deeper salvation from sin. It is
often true still that only through the physical can God open men's
eyes to the spiritual. Thus it should occasion no surprise that Gideon sought a visible and outward sign rather than some inward
assurance and leading. Indeed, the Incarnation itself is, at a higher
and unique level, a reminder that God is pleased to give himself
to us, not through mystical vision, but by taking our flesh and
manifesting himself to us in the nail-marked hands and wounded
side of the Christ.

Not satisfied with one manifestation through the fleece, Gideon
had to try it a second time, but the outcome confirmed the divine
message and sent him out with confidence.

Planning and Spying (7:1-15)

Gideon encamped beside the spring of Harod at the foot of
Mount Gilboa. The Midianites were across the valley to the north,
by the hill of Moreh. The Israelite army numbered 32,000. God
intimated to Gideon that this was too large a number if Israel was
not to vaunt itself on its own prowess in the hour of victory. In
the campaigns of this period, it was God who fought for his peo-

ple, and his was the victory. Hence there must not be sufficient strength in the Israelite band to detract from God's triumph. This is, in some sense, a prefiguring of the deeper and more spiritual truth that we have no power to save ourselves from the tyranny of sin but are wholly dependent upon God's grace. In the deeps of religion we have to learn that God's strength is made perfect through our weakness (see II Cor. 12:9).

Gideon, under divine guidance, dismissed the fearful and timorous warriors, but there were still too many. Then came the water test as a means of eliminating the slothful and of retaining only the alert and watchful. At last a small but compact band of 300 remained. The reference to jars and trumpets in verse 8 is a preparation for Gideon's stratagem described later.

Gideon now began to lay his plans. In a spying expedition he was able to enter the Midianite encampment and to overhear the telling of a dream. The extent of the invasion is indicated by the description of the host as like locusts and of their camels as without number. The dream itself is somewhat obscure. The tent portrayed in it apparently symbolizes the Midianite host, and the cake of barley bread may indicate the agricultural and peasant nature of the Israelite defenders. The interpretation given to the Midianite dreamer by his companion confirmed Gideon's conviction that the Lord was with him. We are told that Gideon worshiped, praising God for this fresh sign of his favor. Thus undergirded, Gideon turned to his task with confidence.

The Rout of Midian (7:16—8:3)

Gideon divided his 300 men into three companies and planned a night surprise attack in which he intended to rout the enemy by fear and panic rather than by armed force. He equipped each of his men with a trumpet and with a jar in which a torch could burn. The point of the strategy was the element of surprise and the psychological effect of the sudden noise of the trumpets and the blaze of light from the torches.

The Hebrew division of the night was into three watches of four hours each. Gideon and his men arrived at the beginning of the middle watch and, at the given signal, carried out their strategy. The panic that ensued was made worse by the thick darkness. Unable to distinguish friend from foe, the Midianites turned on one another and fled in confusion. The three places mentioned in their line of flight are not easily identifiable, but apparently two

lay to the east and one to the west of the Jordan. The rout was
complete, and at this point the men of Naphtali and Asher appear
to have joined the forces of Manasseh. Ephraim came also at the
summons of Gideon, sealing up the Jordan crossings and killing
two Midianite leaders, Oreb ("raven") and Zeeb ("wolf"), whose
heads were brought to Gideon beyond Jordan.

The resentment of the Ephraimites at being summoned so late
is a reminder of the prominent position occupied by Ephraim in
the tribal and political structure. Belonging to the Josephite group,
they occupied a strategic position in the hill country, were prominent in the original invasion, and possessed the central shrine at
Shiloh. To political and religious prestige we must add the point
that later arrival on the battle scene could only mean lesser spoils
of war. By diplomatically minimizing his own efforts and magni-
fying the contribution of the Ephraimites, Gideon managed to ap-
pease the disaffected tribe. He pointed out the fact that to them
belonged the glory of capturing the Midianite chieftains, and
either quoted or formulated a proverb in amelioration of their resentment—"Is not the gleaning of the grapes of Ephraim better
than the vintage of Abiezer?", a saying which magnified them at
the expense of his own tribe.

The Pursuit Beyond Jordan (8:4-21)

Gideon and his three hundred men pursued the fleeing Midianites across Jordan, weary though they themselves were. They ex-
pected help, especially provisions, from their Israelite brethren
across Jordan, but found that the men of Succoth and Penuel, two
cities on the River Jabbok (see Gen. 33:17 and 32:30-31), refused it. These Israelites appear to have been skeptical of any success attending Gideon's pursuit, probably assuming that the Midianite camel bands would just fade away into the desert fastnesses
and it would be beyond Gideon's skill to hunt them out. Undoubtedly, however, there was also some fear of Midianite retaliation, for these Israelites lived on the wrong side of Jordan, in
close proximity to the desert and its nomads. We may even see
here a reflection of the apathy and indifference with which Deborah had earlier charged the Gileadites. Gideon persisted in his
pursuit, leaving the discipline of these non-co-operative Israelites
until his return.

The different names of the chieftains of the Midianites could
indicate that we have here a second tradition. Actually this need

not be the case. Nomads would be at best a loose confederation of tribes and would have many tribal chiefs. Gideon caught up with his fleeing foes at Karkor to the east of the Dead Sea. The number of the fallen indicates how severe the rout had been. Gideon appears to have followed the Midianites by a caravan route east of two trans-Jordanian cities. He caught the Midianites off their guard, and pursued and captured their kings.

Gideon now returned to deal with his own non-co-operating kinsfolk. The reference to "the ascent of Heres" is obscure and the way of return cannot be identified. As he approached Succoth, he captured a young man of the town, from whom he secured the names of the officials and elders. On his arrival at the city Gideon threw back the taunt of the citizens in their face, and "taught" (literally, "threshed") their leaders by thorns and briers. Some suggest that this meant death by torture. The fact that the young man of Succoth "wrote" the names of the city fathers is a reminder that the Hebrews were already practiced in the art of writing, and that we must be careful about describing them as a primitive people. They had already many marks of culture, and were living in the midst of a Canaanite civilization in which writing was an accepted art. Gideon also dealt with Penuel, wrecking its tower and slaying the men of the city. The *lex talionis* (the law of retaliation which stipulated "an eye for an eye and a tooth for a tooth"), in all its relentlessness, governed Hebrew thought in this matter, and possibly here an even cruder spirit of revenge is to be seen.

We come now upon a more fundamental principle in Israelite life, that of blood revenge. Gideon's ruthless pursuit of the two kings had this motive behind it as well as the major concern of delivering Israel. We learn now that the campaign had a blood feud at its center. Zebah and Zalmunnah had slain Gideon's brothers at Tabor, and it was knowledge of this dastardly deed that lay behind his treatment of them. Although desiring to spare them, he declared that this deed spelled their doom. In the end, when his son proved fainthearted, Gideon slew the kings himself. The latter seem coldbloodedly to acknowledge his right to execute them, and to rejoice that, instead of being disgraced by death at the hands of a boy, they were to be slain by the Israelite hero himself. Gideon took as spoil the "crescents" on the camels, of the type still worn today to ward off the "evil eye," and in those days also worn by women as ornaments (see Isa. 3:18).

We find it difficult to understand, much less condone, this
savage act. Nobility of character could have been shown by Gideon in magnanimity toward his victims, and his attitude is not im-
proved by the brutal request he made of his son. We have to remember that Israel was in a historical process of divine encounter,
in which its lower standards of morality and its misunderstanding
of the divine will were being challenged and corrected by successive divine interventions. Man was not yet ready for the full revelation of the Incarnation.

Kingship and the Ephod—the Closing Summary (8:22-35)

Gideon's success led Israel, or at least the portion of it particularly affected by his triumph, to turn its mind to the thought of
kingship. For the first time in Israel's history, we have an attempt
to establish an hereditary monarchy. Gideon's strength and leadership singled him out as the focal point of Israel's hope. He was
manifestly one on whom the Spirit of the Lord had come, and the
future of the people seemed bound up with him. Gideon's refusal
of the kingship for himself and his son was accompanied by an
affirmation of Israel's traditional position. Hitherto and throughout the period of the judges, Israel was a theocracy ruled over directly by God, who used certain distinctive personalities at appropriate times to effect his kingly rule. As we shall see subsequently
in First Samuel, this tradition persisted long, even though the desire for a human monarch was growing along with it. Hosea reflected this tradition in the eighth century B.C. when he declared
that God gave Israel a king in his anger and took him away in his
wrath (Hosea 13:10-11). In this tradition, the earthly kingship
was a sign of sin and rebellion against the kingly rule of God himself. This was echoed in Gideon's words. He would not usurp the
rights of God who had empowered him.

Gideon, on his part, made a request of his followers for the
golden earrings taken as spoil from the Midianites. With these he
made an ephod and set it up in his native city of Ophrah. The
word "ephod" had a diversity of meanings in Old Testament
times. Later it seems to have meant either a priestly vestment or
an appurtenance holding the Urim and Thummim (the objects
used in the casting of sacred lots) and thus possessing oracular
significance. Here, however, it seems to mean an image and thus
an idol. It may have been a vestment so heavily weighted with
gold that it stood erect, but "idol" seems much more consonant

with the fact that Gideon is said here to have initiated an evil tradition, so that the citizens of Ophrah "played the harlot after it,"
a phrase used to describe idolatrous worship. The making of
graven images was expressly forbidden in wilderness days, according to the Mosaic Decalogue. In this story we find at least one
source of idolatry, to which a pagan Canaanite environment may
well have contributed. The making of this ephod was regarded as
the cause of the disaster which subsequently overtook Gideon and
his family, as the term "a snare" indicates.

The chapter closes with an account of Gideon's family in which
Abimelech is introduced as his son by his concubine in Shechem.
Gideon died at a ripe old age, and, after his death, the cycle of
paganism and Baal worship returned once more in the life of
Israel. If the resurgence of paganism at this point was a new
phase, then it may be that the use of the ephod during Gideon's
lifetime was not a form of pagan worship, but that the ephod was
regarded as a visible sign of God's presence. We notice the mention of Baal-berith, "Lord of a covenant," who was the local
deity of the Canaanites at Shechem. The Israelites forgot God and
even forgot their debt to Gideon, for they failed to show kindness
to his family.

The King of Shechem (9:1-6)

The story of Abimelech, in chapter 9, is significant in many
ways. It demonstrates that the Canaanites still abode in the land
and had not been wiped out. Such Canaanites appear to have retained many of the large cities, but here we are shown how one
such city, Shechem, came under Israelite control. The story shows
how the inhabitants of the land and the Hebrew invaders became
fused together.

The history of Shechem is of interest. It was a city in the midst
of the tribal area of Ephraim between Mount Gerizim to the
south and Mount Ebal on the north. It had strategic importance,
since it formed an easy pass between the coastal plain of the
Mediterranean Sea and the Jordan Valley. It appears to have
figured in pre-Israelite history and to have been connected with
the historical vicissitudes of the patriarchs. Both Abraham (Gen.
12:6) and Jacob (Gen. 33:18) had connections with it, while
the tragic story of the rape of Dinah by the young prince of Shechem carries some memory of tribal history in which the group
of Israelites descended from Dinah disappeared and disaster be-

fell the Canaanites at Shechem (Gen. 34). When the Israelite
invaders entered central Canaan they seem early to have formed
some association with the Shechemites. Joseph was buried there
in a piece of ground purchased from the inhabitants by Jacob; it
was the scene of Joshua's farewell address; and there the Covenant of Sinai was renewed by the tribal confederation which was
soon to be victorious over the land (Joshua 24). Yet Shechem
remained in Canaanite hands. The fact that its god was named
Baal-berith, "Lord of a covenant," suggests that there may have
been some affinity between its religion and the Covenant faith
of Israel. This would account for the fact that the ceremony of
Covenant renewal took place there. Gideon intermarried with
a Shechemite woman, and his victory over the marauding Midianites certainly benefited the Canaanite inhabitants of that city
as much as it did the Israelites.

Abimelech's mother is described as an inhabitant of Shechem
and as Gideon's "concubine." The latter term covers a type of
marriage in which the wife remained in her own clan and was
occasionally visited by her husband. The children of such a marriage belonged to the wife's clan. This partly accounts for the fact
that the Shechemites were prepared to make Abimelech king.
Another reason was a long tradition of Canaanite kingship in
general and at Shechem in particular, where the line of rule went
back to the Hamor with whom Abraham had dealings. We can
therefore understand why the men of Shechem fell in so readily
with Abimelech's plans. Indeed, it may be that Abimelech's Canaanite mother was of the influential family of Hamor. Her kins-
men evidently were men of influence and could make use of the
temple treasury. Making capital out of his father's reputation and
appealing to the Shechemites on the ground of common blood,
Abimelech secured help at the expense of the funds appropriated
to the worship of Baal-berith. He gathered a band around him
and slew all his rival brothers except Jotham, who managed to
escape. The reference to the brothers' being all slain at one stone
might suggest that this was a sacrificial slaying.

We note how the fusion between Canaanites and Israelites
was already taking place through intermarriage and how separate
traditions were being interwoven, so that before long the two
groups were indistinguishable. The worship of the Lord was celebrated often at once-pagan shrines; the forms of pagan ritual and
ceremony were taken over and adapted by the religion of the God

of Israel; and the traditions of Moses, the Exodus and the desert
wanderings, the patriarchs and the promise, became a part of the
common stock of an increasingly homogeneous people.

Jotham's Fable (9:7-21)

Jotham, the one brother who had escaped from the slaughter,
climbed to the height of Mount Gerizim above Shechem, and
harangued the populace with a fable. The trees offer a kingship in turn to their various members. The olive refuses it because of its distinctive service of supplying the oil of anointing
for kings, religious leaders, and sacrificial feasts. The fig tree de-
clines it because of its important function in providing men with
necessary food. The vine rejects it because it must go on producing its wine. At last the trees turn to the lowly and useless
bramble, little better than a weed. The bramble greedily and
arrogantly accepts, even threatening those who had offered it
an honor which it does not deserve, for it may harbor a fire
which could bring low even the cedars of Lebanon. Obviously the
refusal of the nobler trees represents Gideon's rejection of the
kingship, while the valueless bramble in its arrogance stands for
Abimelech, who had neither the wisdom nor the capacity for
kingship.

Jotham's interpretation follows. As we have seen, the implication of the fable is that Abimelech is not a man of integrity and
leadership to whom men can give their confidence. In the interpretation, Jotham turned on the lords of Shechem themselves,
arraigning them for the treatment of Gideon's sons in return for
his victorious leadership, and for installing the unworthy Abimelech. If they had done this in good faith, they would soon be
disillusioned. That good faith was understandable in the case of
Gideon, but not in the case of Abimelech. The result would be
disaster for both of them. Having invoked his curse, Jotham fled
from the lofty eminence, which he had chosen because it made
possible an easy escape. He went to Beer, an unidentified location.

The Rebellion Under Gaal (9:22-41)

Abimelech ruled three years amid increasing discord. The
reference to all Israel must not be taken literally. Abimelech
ruled only over the area around Shechem, and there is no indication of a widely extended kingship. We learn that he resided
at Arumah (9:41), that he governed Shechem through a governor

Zebul, and also that he lost his life in an expedition to Thebez
(9:50). Although the site of Arumah is unknown, Thebez was
only about twelve miles northeast of Shechem. This was a localized kingship and as yet there was no national solidarity.

After three years the Shechemites rose in revolt. We are told
that God sent an evil spirit between them and Abimelech. This
is a Hebrew way of describing the advent of a demonic element
in any situation. In like manner Saul's madness is later ascribed
to an evil spirit (I Sam. 16:14). Behind the phrase, however,
there are psychological and theological implications. Hebrew
psychology was built on the idea that human personality could
be invaded by windlike spirit forces, and that abnormal characteristics, good or evil, were due to such possession. Hebrew theol-
ogy saw God as the ground of all life and its manifold experiences. It tended to ignore secondary causes and lead everything
back directly to God, a somewhat natural tendency in all religious faith that is conscious of absolute dependence upon a
creator. As the revelation to Israel became richer and the
emphasis on man's sin and freedom became central, light was
shed in the midst of the mystery. The Cross and the Empty
Tomb penetrate the heart of the mystery and remind us that
God accepts responsibly the presence of evil in his world and
deals with it. We may even say that God permits evil and over-
rules it for his purpose, but in saying that he permits it, are we
not simply repeating in a more sophisticated and less challenging
way what the author of Judges meant by the phrase "God sent
an evil spirit"? In the last resort, all things, even misused freedom, lie within God's will, and the Cross is the measure of his
gracious acceptance of this and of his dealing with it.

The story sees the evil spirit as God's judgment on Abimelech
for his treachery. The men of Shechem acted treacherously toward Abimelech. They ambushed caravans passing along the
caravan route and thus made life in the area insecure. It has
been suggested that Abimelech had levied a toll as the price of
safe transit and that the acts of the Shechemites threatened his
source of revenue. Before long the discontent grew as opponents
of Abimelech found their way to Shechem, especially Gaal the
son of Ebed and his kinsfolk. Soon an organized conspiracy was
on foot, and open revolt flared up. At the close of the grape
harvest, Gaal harangued the lords of Shechem and gained their
support for revolt. At this point we learn that Abimelech did

not rule from Shechem but had put in a governor, Zebul. The skillful speaker emphasized the fact that once Abimelech and Gideon had served the sons of Hamor, and raised the question, "Why then should we serve him?" Gaal openly challenged Abimelech and implied that he himself ought to have authority.

Zebul, the governor, sent notification of the revolt to Abimelech and suggested a way of dealing with it. Abimelech and his men were to surround the city at night and launch a surprise attack at sunrise. This Abimelech did, dividing his force into four companies. Meanwhile Zebul simulated friendship for Gaal and arranged for him to attack Abimelech under the least favorable conditions. He lured Gaal to the gate and, when the rebel leader saw the forces of Abimelech descending upon the city from the mountain fastnesses, persuaded him to go out from the city and join battle. The strategy seems to have been to get Gaal outside the protection of the city defenses. The rebels were routed by Abimelech, and those who escaped were dealt with by Zebul. Abimelech returned to Arumah and left Zebul in charge.

The Destruction of Shechem (9:42-49)

It is not clear whether this is a different version of the preceding narrative or an account of a later incident. Some of the details in this story, such as the battle in the fields and the mention of the gate, may suggest that it is another version of the same events. On the other hand, the narrative may well describe a final campaign against the city, the cause of which has been lost in the obscurity of history. The story is so linked to the preceding one that immediate proximity in time is suggested by the phrase "on the following day," but this must be accepted with caution. Whatever happened, and when, the story records the total destruction of Shechem—the wiping out of its inhabitants and the razing of its buildings. The statement that Abimelech "razed the city and sowed it with salt" has a parallel in the Annals of Tiglath-pileser I, who reports of a city which he razed: "and salt thereon I sowed." The idea is that the perpetual desolation of the city is thereby assured. The Tower of Shechem appears to have been situated apart from the city itself. It, too, was razed, and the Shechemites who had sought refuge in the temple of the "Lord of a covenant" found that this did not avail them. The whole was burned by fire and the people were destroyed.

The Death of Abimelech (9:50-57)

The revolt against Abimelech still persisted at Thebez, twelve miles northeast of Shechem. The king marched against it and met his doom. As he besieged the stronghold in the city, a woman on top of the tower cast down a millstone that crushed him. His arrogance was manifested to the end in his command to his armor-bearer to kill him, lest it be remembered that he was killed by a woman.

So Jotham's curse was fulfilled, and the first Israelite effort at kingship proved abortive. The editor of Judges sees the story as a manifestation of divine judgment on Abimelech for his treachery to his brethren and on the Shechemites for their weakness in co-operating with Abimelech in his sin.

The Minor Judges—Tola and Jair (10:1-5)

We find little of religious interest in these verses. The two judges mentioned, Tola and Jair, are not linked with any specific enemies of the Israelites. Both names occur in genealogical tables earlier—Tola in Genesis 46:13 and Numbers 26:23; Jair in Numbers 32:41 and Deuteronomy 3:14. These tables associate Tola with Issachar and Jair with Manasseh. Jair in this passage is termed a Gileadite, but Numbers 32:39-41 links Jair the Manassite with the conquest of Gilead, and both Numbers 32:41 and Deuteronomy 3:14 associate him with Havvoth-jair (the tent villages of Jair), as does our text. This at least indicates the locale of these figures, but it is useless to speculate further. Only names and trifling memories have remained. The editor gives the years of judgeship and other details in conformity with his customary formula, and indicates that Jair was a man of substance by referring to the fact that his thirty sons each rode on an ass.

Jephthah the Gileadite (10:6—12:7)

The New Period of Oppression (10:6-16)

Once more a cycle of oppression returned. This time the dramatis personae were the Ammonites instead of the Midianites, and the peoples of Gilead, Judah, Benjamin, and Ephraim rather than those farther north. The usual editorial formula in verses

6-9 traces the oppression to the people's apostasy. Again they forgot the Lord and went after the fertility gods of the Canaanites. Once again God's wrath descended on them and they were delivered into the hands of the Philistines and the Ammonites. The latter, who dwelt beyond Gilead to the east of Jordan, began by oppressing the Gileadites, the Hebrew people east of Jordan, but soon extended their depredations into the areas occupied by Judah, Benjamin, and Ephraim.

The reference to the Philistines at this point seems out of place, since Jephthah does not appear to have been concerned with them. There is no similar introduction to the Samson story, however, so the editorial summary at this point may include the Philistines in order to cover the Samson epic also in the same general terms.

In verses 10-16 there is a dramatic dialogue between God and Israel. Israel confesses its apostasy, only to be reminded of other divine deliverances from its foes which had not hindered it from its present sin. God dramatically calls on Israel to find its help in the gods whom it has chosen, but the nation acknowledges its guilt and continues to call on the Lord for deliverance. At last its rejection of the Baals brings down the divine compassion; God could not endure the continued oppression of his people. The list of oppressors here cited includes many who do not seem to have operated in Israel's history before Jephthah's time. The Ammonites were the current oppressors; as we have seen, the Philistine invasion became an issue later in Samson's time; the Maonites belong to the time of Jehoshaphat; there does not seem to have been a separate oppression by the Amalekites, although earlier they were associated with the Moabites and the Midianites; the Phoenicians likewise do not appear to have been a problem at this time. This list of nations corresponds with the list of foreign deities in verse 6, and would appear to be an editorial summary reflecting the conditions under the monarchy when it was written, rather than the state of affairs during Jephthah's judgeship.

The Deliverer and His Challenge (10:17—11:28)

The Ammonites assembled to do battle in Gilead. The Israelites gathered at Mizpah, whose site has not been identified. Mysteriously, however, Israel had no battle leader. It was declared that such a one, if he could be found, should become head over all the inhabitants of Gilead. Verses 17 and 18, which record this, appear to be a general summary of the situation, since Jephthah is boldly introduced in 11:1, with no reference to the statement contained in the previous verses, and the theme of war with the Ammonites is raised once more in 11:4-5, this time with mention of Jephthah.

In 11:1-3, we are given information about Jephthah himself. He was the son of a harlot and thus genealogically fatherless. His mother was neither a lawful wife nor a concubine. Hence in the place of a father, the name of the land of his birth is substituted. Gilead was the father of Jephthah. As a bastard, Jephthah had no hereditary rights. His half-brothers drove him out, so that he became the leader of a lawless band in the land of Tob, now thought to be in the neighborhood of Ramoth-gilead.

In their plight, the elders of Gilead recalled Jephthah from his outlawry to invite him to be their leader against the Ammonites. He discomfited them by the brutally frank query as to why they should suddenly reverse their attitude toward him. Characteristics which led to outlawry in peacetime had become valuable in wartime. Trouble and crisis often make us see qualities in people that we do not see in times of peace. The elders repeated their conviction that only a victorious leader in battle was qualified to be chief of the land in time of peace, and implied that Jephthah's skill in the former made him their inevitable choice. He accepted their double offer and they swore to keep their side of the compact. The Lord was witness or hearer of their oath. Jephthah's acceptance of leadership, provided he was successful in battle, and the corresponding commitment of the elders of Gilead were ratified before the Lord at Mizpah. Here there seems to be indicated some mutual covenantal rite between the erstwhile outlaw and the elders at the local shrine. Jephthah, we read, "spoke all his words before the LORD at Mizpah."

Jephthah now inquired of the Ammonites their motives in making war, only to be told that Israel took from them the land east of the Jordan, from the border of Moab northward, and that it should be restored to them as its rightful owners.

In reply, the Israelite leader argued for Israel's right to the land east of the Jordan. He contended that when Israel entered Canaan she took no land from Moab or Ammon but respected their rights; that when Edom and Moab refused permission for Israel to pass through their territory, the Hebrew people detoured around those regions (Num. 20:14-21; 21:11-13), even taking care not to trespass in Moab by camping beyond its boundary, the River Arnon; that when they asked permission to pass through the land of the Amorites, Sihon refused such peaceful passage, so that they forcibly took possession of his land (see Num. 21:21—22:1). The point of the last reference is that this was part of the area now under dispute, southern Gilead north of the Moabite border. Thus Israel held Sihon's land by right of conquest. Jephthah argued that Israel's God had fought for it, and hence that God had dispossessed this land for Israel and given it into the possession of his people. After all, the god of the Ammonites had given their land into their possession, so why should they dispute what Israel's God had given to it? We notice two things here. The first is the mistaken name of the Ammonite deity. "Chemosh" (vs. 24) was the god of Moab rather than of Ammon. This confusion may have been a mistake of later editors. The second feature is the emphasis on the reality of the other deities. In Jephthah's speech Israel's God is thought of as existing alongside the gods of the other nations. There is little doubt that monotheism, the faith in one universal deity, was implicit in the revelation to Moses and that Moses himself had the rudiments of such a faith; but contact with other nations had prevented Israel from sharing the vision of the great wilderness leader. Other gods were tied to national territory, and, at this stage, Israel at times conceived of God in the same way, although the deeper vision of God's might and activity kept breaking through.

The implication of Jephthah's argument so far was that Ammon's claim to Gilead was unjustified. He now turned to previous attempts to hinder Israel's victorious progress. Balak of Moab had not succeeded and Ammon had no better claim to the conquered land than he. Furthermore, why had Ammon waited three hundred years before asserting its rights to the territory? The two places mentioned, Heshbon and Aroer, are situated in Gilead east of Jordan and north of the Moabite border at Arnon. We note that the period of 300 years actually fits into the length of the period of the judges so far covered in the book. Until the beginning of the Ammonite oppression, the figures add up to 301 years. Ammon was in the wrong, argued Jephthah. If the Ammonites wanted to make war over the issue, then God would decide between them and Israel.

Jephthah's Vow and Victory (11:29-33)

The charismatic element now enters into the situation. The Spirit of the Lord came upon Jephthah. His message rejected, he stirred up the men of Manasseh and Gilead for war. Apparently they gathered at the shrine at Mizpah, where Jephthah vowed that if God vouchsafed victory, Jephthah would offer as a burnt offering whoever first crossed the threshold of his home to greet him on his return. Evidently a human sacrifice was here implied. A great blessing from God seemed to demand a supreme sacrifice in return, and Israelite custom was still at the level when human or child sacrifice was not unknown. The patriarchal story of Abraham's offering of Isaac and the provision of the ram as a substitute reflects the period when men were learning that God did not require a human life at their hands (Gen. 22:9-14). Jephthah is to be judged here by the standards of his time and not by ours. At least he was giving to God what he had. He must have known that his daughter was a real possibility, since, according to custom, the women of the house came forth to greet a returning victor (see I Sam. 18:6). God demands our best—this at least was recognized, but with misunderstanding of its significance.

The victory over the Ammonites was complete. The Lord delivered them into Israel's hand, an indication that this was regarded as a holy war in which God fought for and with his people. The same implication lies in the emphasis on the charismatic nature of Jephthah's leadership.

Jephthah's Return (11:34-40)

As with Miriam's greeting and at Saul's victorious return (Exod. 15:20; I Sam. 18:6), so in Jephthah's case, he was greeted by the women of his household with timbrels and dances. His only child, a daughter, came first to greet him in this way, and the terrible nature of his vow dawned on him. His predicament was that he could not take back the vow, an indication that it came out of a deeply religious emotion. We need to remember the Hebrew realism involved here. A man's words, if uttered in high seriousness, became extensions of his own personality and carried something of himself in them. Should he fail to fulfill them, then his own personal integrity would be at stake (see Deut. 23:21-22). His daughter, with a noble simplicity, recognized Jephthah's dilemma. God had given him triumph, and he must fulfill his vow. Let him grant her two months to bewail her virginity; that is, to lament that she was to die unmarried and childless. Again we note the Hebrew realism, for in those early days, to die childless meant to have no perpetuity beyond death. At best, personal survival after death was but a shadowy one in Sheol, the one abode of the dead which embraced every family grave. Real immortality lay in the extension of personality down through time in one's offspring. Hence the grief of Rachel weeping for her children has a double bitterness (Jer. 31:15; Matt. 2:18), as does the case of Jephthah's daughter.

The writer with fine restraint implies that the vow was carried out and the sacrifice made. This noble story, despite its primitive background and uncivilized overtones, has inspired poems by Byron and Tennyson. But, long before this, it had left its mark on Israel's history. When, in after years, the pagan ceremony of weeping for Tammuz (Ezek. 8:14), a god of spring and fertility, had inspired an annual retreat of the women of Israel, the true motivation of this ceremony appears to have been covered up by the identification of it with the annual remembrance of Jephthah's daughter. With all of Jephthah's limitations and lack of ethical vision, his deep sense of obligation to God colors this story, as does the piety of his daughter.

Jephthah's Repulse of the Jealous Ephraimites (12:1-7)

The Ephraimites now caused trouble with Jephthah, as they had done previously with Gideon (8:1-3). They felt slighted by not being included in Jephthah's campaign and threatened to burn down his house. In armed strength they confronted Jephthah at Zaphon, east of Jordan. Gideon had appeased the Ephraimites, but Jephthah resorted to the way of battle. He began, however, by implying that their help had been invoked and that their failure had left the Gileadites alone to fight the Ammonites. His speech apparently failed to convince the jealous Ephraimites, for Jephthah summoned his men to do battle and routed his fellow Hebrews. By capturing the fords at the Jordan, which formed the boundary of Ephraim, he was able to halt his enemy countrymen as they sought to cross and return to their homeland. The device by which he identified the Ephraimites was the test of pronunciation—the Ephraimites pronounced "sh" as "s," and the word chosen for the test was "Shibboleth" ("stream"). Many Ephraimites must have been slain by their own kinsfolk.

The usual closing summary records Jephthah's judgeship as lasting six years. It is evident that his work and rule were confined to Gilead and thus covered the limited area east of Jordan, not all Israel.

The Minor Judges—Ibzan, Elon, and Abdon (12:8-15)

Ibzan's name occurs only here. The Bethlehem with which he is associated was probably the town of that name in Zebulun. The size of his family is indicative of his wealth, but, apart from the customary editorial formula, we have no other information. Elon was likewise of Zebulun, and references in Genesis 46:14 and Numbers 26:26 link the name with this tribe. Abdon is a name occurring elsewhere (for example, I Chron. 8:23). He was associated with Pirathon which, according to I Chronicles 27:14, was in Ephraim. The size of his family and the fact that his sons and grandsons all rode asses are measures of his material substance. The reference to Amalekite territory in Ephraim is obscure in meaning.

Samson and the Philistines (13:1—16:31)

The Message of the Angel (13:1-7)

Once again the editor repeats his formula of sin and judgment, a turning to God and the raising of a deliverer. This time the oppressors were the Philistines, a seafaring people from the Mediterranean lands who, about this time, invaded the coastal strip of Palestine. We know that these "peoples of the sea" invaded Egypt in the time of Rameses III (about 1200 B.C.), and that shortly after being driven off they sought settlement on the Shephelah. They soon established themselves in walled cities, making armed raids into the Israelite territory and causing trouble down to the time of David.

Manoah is described as a Danite, living on the borders of Judah west of Jerusalem. This is an indication of the original southerly location of the tribe of Dan, before its northward migration (chs. 17 and 18). Like Sarah, the wife of Abraham, Manoah's wife was barren. Like the patriarchal couple, Manoah and his wife were visited by an angel of the Lord. We have already, in the case of Gideon, discussed the significance of this

visitation, pointing out that it was not an angel in the modern
sense, but a divinely sent messenger who was regarded as an
extension of the personality of God, and, in greater or lesser
degree, was identified with God himself. The angel in the case
of Abraham is described in more supernatural terms. In this story
Manoah's wife describes the messenger to her husband as a
"man of God" who was as an "angel of God." The phrase "man
of God" customarily described a prophet. Thus the angel may
have been a divinely sent human visitant who, like the prophets,
was for the time being identified with, and the mouthpiece of,
the God of Israel (see the story of Gideon). The promise of a son
was accompanied by a description of him as a Nazirite. A
Nazirite was a man set apart and dedicated to God, distinguished
from his fellows by abstinence from strong drink, by letting his
hair grow long, and by keeping out of contact with dead bodies.
These rules are enumerated in Numbers 6. Such Nazirites might
be so dedicated for a limited time or for life. This child was
apparently to be subjected to a lifetime vow. The baby so born
was to be the promised deliverer.

Manoah's Request and the Sacrifice (13:8-23)

Manoah prayed for a return visit of the "man," the theophanic
messenger, that the parents might learn how to rear the promised
child. This is a reminder, incidentally, of what true piety should
mean in a home and in the birth and nurture of a child. The
messenger returned to the wife, but this time she summoned her
husband to his presence. The instructions about diet indicate that
the boy was to be a Nazirite.

At this point we again are impressed by the parallels between
this story and the patriarchal narratives. Manoah's behavior is
similar to that of Abraham in Genesis 18. Manoah desired to
honor his guest with a meal, still assuming him to be a man and
unaware of the true nature of his visitant. At this point we encounter what may be called the supernatural element in the
story. The visitor refused the proffered meal but suggested instead
a burnt offering to the Lord. Manoah now requested the name of
his messenger that he might do him proper honor when the
promise was fulfilled and the child was born. To this request
there came the reply "wonderful," which means in the Hebrew
"beyond comprehension," "superhuman." Manoah began to realize that this was more than a human being and was rather a

superhuman, so he offered a sacrifice to the God who worked wondrously, who was in essence superhuman. As the flame of the burnt offering flared up, the visitant mysteriously ascended in it and disappeared from sight. At this point Manoah came to a full realization of the nature of the visitation. He and his wife had seen God, and they could not live. We note at this point that the angel is identified with God and regarded as an extension of God himself. Manoah's wife was more balanced than he, and declared logically that God's acceptance of their sacrifice meant that they would be spared.

Samson's Birth and Inspiration (13:24-25)

The child was duly born and named Samson, which means "little sun." The name need not associate Samson with some sun cult. It appears to have been a common proper name in early Canaan along with other combinations in which the word for "sun" occurs. There is every evidence that the Israelites borrowed many names from their Canaanite neighbors, and so here, in all probability.

We are told that the Lord blessed Samson, and that the Spirit of the Lord first took possession of him at Mahaneh-dan ("Camp of Dan"). He, like the other judges before him, was a charismatic personality whose feats of strength and prowess in war were ascribed to the presence in him of the windlike "Spirit of the Lord," which could endow its recipients with abnormal power and wisdom. This Spirit became an irresistible urge in Samson, moving him to extraordinary feats of strength. The child of promise thus received his full endowment.

Samson Falls in Love (14:1-4)

Samson's youth is passed over, and we next meet him falling in love with a Philistine. This indicates that, up to this point, the coastal invaders and the Israelites were not in open hostility. This was a period of settling down and consolidation, a fact which is supported by archaeological evidence. Customarily the Hebrew parents made the choice of the bride for a son, as well as the financial arrangements for securing her. Here Samson made the choice and sought the co-operation of his parents; they protested, however, against his choice of a bride from among the Philistines. The editor implies that even this choice was in the divine strategy, for it would provide an occasion against the Philistines.

The Adventure with the Lion (14:5-9)

The protest of his parents notwithstanding, Samson went down to Timnah to pursue his objective. All versions put the verb "come" in the singular, and thus suggest that Samson went alone, the mention of his father and his mother as accompanying him being a later addition. Samson was now determined upon the kind of marriage in which his parents accepted no responsibility, and the presence of his parents was thus unnecessary. This peculiar type of marriage did not involve a marriage price paid to the bride's father by the father of the bridegroom, and the wife continued to dwell in her father's house, there to be visited periodically by her husband.

On the way, the roar of a lion attracted Samson, who, possessed of an abnormal strength by the presence of the Spirit of God, tore the lion asunder by sheer brute force, leaving the carcass by the way. A later visit to his future bride brought Samson once more by the lion's body, which had now been possessed by a swarm of bees and filled with honeycomb. Both elements in this story—the slaying of the lion and the swarm of bees occupying a dead body—are to be found elsewhere in hero legends. Hercules and Polydemas are credited with slaying lions with their bare hands. Virgil and Herodotus connected swarms of bees with carcasses. Indeed, there seems to have been an ancient idea that bees were generated by putrefying flesh. Such parallels need not call the historicity of this story into question. The location of the bees and their honey remained a closely guarded secret which Samson did not communicate even to his parents and which provided the basis for his subsequent riddle.

The Wedding Feast and the Riddle (14:10-20)

As a preliminary to his wedding, Samson entertained the young men at a feast where he propounded his riddle and challenged them to solve it within the seven days of the feast. Unaware of the circumstances that lay behind the bare statement of the riddle, they strove unavailingly for a solution over a period of three days. The wager involved a considerable amount of apparel which neither side could afford to lose. The young men were provided by the Timnahites as the companions of the bridegroom and thus had no long friendship for or loyalty to Samson. They therefore approached his bride, threatening to

burn down her parental home and her in it, unless she found
the answer. This threatened calamity was serious enough to call
forth all her woman's wiles, including tears. If Samson loved
her, she pleaded, surely he would tell her his secret. At last, worn
out by her importunities, Samson told her the solution, unaware
of either the threat to her or her intended treachery. When the
young men came up with the answer to the riddle, at the very
last moment, Samson's rage knew no bounds. He answered the
men in a jingle of the same form as his riddle, and, disgusted
with his wife's treachery, left her, the marriage unconsummated.
(This is the meaning of the phrase "before the sun went down"
which can also be translated "before he entered the room to take
his bride.") Once more an access of strength, because of his
Spirit-possession, enabled him to overpower thirty Philistines
and despoil them of their festal garments that he might pay his
debt to the Philistines of Timnah. Meanwhile his bride was con-
soled by being given as wife to the best man, for otherwise
Samson's wrathful exit would have brought disgrace upon her.
Samson himself returned to his father's house.

Samson's Return and Revenge (15:1-8)

Samson relented and sought to return to his erstwhile wife.
As was customary in such a form of marriage, he took with him
the present of a kid, only to discover that his bride had already
been given to another man. The father attempted to placate
Samson by offering him his younger daughter and thereby acknowledging his error. Samson, however, was not satisfied. His
method of revenge was to let loose in the grainfields three hundred foxes with burning firebrands attached to the tails of each
pair. The resulting destruction of the Philistine grain crop led
the Philistines to avenge themselves by burning Samson's wife
and her father. Samson now carried the fierce vendetta further
by slaughtering yet other Philistines. He then fled and hid in a
cleft of rock somewhere near his home.

Samson and the Philistines at Lehi (15:9-20)

Samson had taken refuge on the borders of Judah, and thither
the Philistines pursued him, threatening the Judahites if Samson
was not handed over. The story implies that the men of Judah
were secretly on his side, but that they were under no tribal
obligation to him since he was a Danite. They went in strength

to secure his submission—a testimony to Samson's reputation—
and the hero gave himself up without resistance. The Judahites
bound him and delivered him over to his enemies at Lehi,
whither the raiding Philistines had come. The name "Lehi" is
here used in anticipation, since evidently this name was the result
of Samson's exploit. The Spirit of the Lord came on Samson
with power; he burst his bonds and slew the Philistines with
the jawbone of an ass, an exploit paralleled in the story of
Shamgar (Judges 3:31) and of Shamnah (II Sam. 23:11-12).
We note that the latter slaying also took place at Lehi. Samson's
effort left him exhausted, and, in response to his prayer, the
Lord caused a spring to issue forth by cleaving a hollow stone
(compare Moses and Israel in the wilderness, Exod. 17).

The Gates of Gaza (16:1-3)

There is no effort on the part of the editor of Judges to gloss
over Samson's moral weakness, nor does he call in question the
relation between Samson's sexual misadventures and his possession of the Spirit. We have to remember, of course, that in these
earlier times the idea of the Spirit of God had not received much
moral content but was understood more in terms of physical
strength and mental skill. The fact that the editor, himself under
the moral influence of the prophetic testimony, should have included the details is a reminder that he sought to be fair to the
tradition.

Samson, heedless of past experience, got into the toils of another woman, and found himself beset by the Philistine inhabitants of Gaza. Waiting for him while he visited the harlot, they
barred the gates of the city to prevent his escape. At midnight, Samson issued forth, carried away the gates of Gaza to
the top of a distant hill, and left his enemies frustrated once
more. Gaza was the outpost of the Philistine invasion and on
the edge of the Israelite hill country.

Samson and Delilah (16:4-22)

Once again Samson showed his weakness for women. This
time his charmer was probably an Israelite, for she had a Semitic
name and lived in a village near his birthplace, Zorah. The
name of the village, Sorek, suggests that it was a grape center
offering a variety of grapes. Israelite or Philistine, this woman,
Delilah, was certainly under Philistine influence, and prepared

to accept a large bribe to do the work of Samson's enemies. She
undertook to discover the secret of Samson's strength, evidently
regarded as of magical origin and requiring the right magical
treatment. Three times Delilah sought to inveigle Samson into
betraying his secret, and three times he deceived her. Binding
him with bowstrings and with new ropes did not prove of any
avail. When he suggested that the seven locks of his hair be
woven into the web on a loom and made tight with a pin, she
tried again, and again found that she had been deceived. Then,
in a moment of weakness and worn out by her importunity,
Samson gave away his secret—his strength lay in his unshaven
hair, kept long from birth by the Nazirite vow. Delilah swiftly
betrayed him to the Philistines and had his locks of hair sheared
off, thus taking away his strength. Samson's enemies made sure
of their foe this time. They put out his eyes, bound him with
brazen fetters, and took him down to Gaza, depositing him in
the prison. The practice of blinding captives appears also in I
Samuel 11:2 and II Kings 25:7. After a time, the hero's hair
began to grow again and his phenomenal strength began to return.

The End of Samson (16:23-31)

The Philistines celebrated Samson's capture at a religious festival, offering thanks to their god, Dagon, who had delivered
them. Presumably there was some lapse of time before the feast
was held, since Samson's hair had grown again.

Dagon was originally a Semitic deity, associated with Baal
and having a place in Mesopotamian religion from early days.
He was worshiped by the Canaanites at Ugarit, and appears to
have been adopted by the Philistines, who made him their chief
god at Ashdod (I Sam. 5:1-7). The temple of Dagon is described
as resting on pillars. This kind of architecture characterized the
palaces and temples of Crete, and its description here supports
the idea that the Philistines came from that island.

The blinded hero was set between the twin pillars that supported the temple, and having been assisted in locating them by
his youthful attendant, brought them down and with them the
temple itself. Thus he involved himself and his captors in a common destruction, destroying more Philistines in his death than
during his life.

The story is far from edifying. The origin of Samson's

strength is sought partly in the charismatic aspect of his personality, and partly in the quasi-magical idea of his unshorn hair.
Samson is possessed by the Spirit of God and yet shows himself
a weakling at the level of sexual temptation. Even his Nazirite
vow seems to have been only partly sustained, since wine and
strong drink flowed at the wedding feast and his slaying of the
Philistines brought him into contact with dead bodies. Moreover, his final disaster is not ascribed to his moral failure but
to his breaking a legal ordinance about his hair. It has well
been said that the story is retained more as warning than example, for it does show the working out of judgment in man's
life. It is also a reminder that God can use even evil and sin to
be executants of his judgment and the agents of his deliverance.

APPENDIX: THE STORY OF DAN AND THE WAR WITH BENJAMIN

Judges 17:1—21:25

The Migration of Dan and the Story of Its Sanctuary (17:1—18:31)

The history of the tribe of Dan is one of the obscure problems of the early period. It is clear from Joshua 19:40-46 that
the Danites once lived in the south of Canaan in land which
later was assigned to Judah (see Joshua 15:33, 45, 56). Yet
they must have moved from this location to their northern home
quite early, for the Song of Deborah places them in the north
(Judges 5:17). It is true that there is an enigmatic reference
to Dan in the Samson story (Judges 13:25; 18:12) which suggests a southern location, but the "Camp of Dan" may refer
to a pocket of Danites left behind after the northward migration. Evidently Amorite pressure early forced the tribe out of its
own home, and thus the story in this appendix is chronologically
prior to many of the judgeships recorded before it.

Actually these two chapters are mainly concerned with the
history of the famous sanctuary which the Danites built in their
new city of Dan in the north. We are dealing here with an old
tradition and a period when imageless worship was not universally accepted. The story is valuable for its insight into early

Israelite religious practice and also into the beginnings of a Hebrew priesthood.

Micah and His Image (17:1-6)

Micah was a countryman dwelling in the hill country of Ephraim to the north of Jerusalem. He had stolen some silver from his mother, and was moved to confess his crime when he heard her curse against the thief. Hebrew words spoken with high seriousness were thought of in an objective sense.

Scholars have found some difficulty with the arrangement of the text in verses 2 and 3, and the usual interpretation is that Micah's mother, prior to his theft of the silver, had already dedicated it to the Lord, so that the curse on the thief was particularly virulent since he had taken what by right belonged to God. This means that we should read the second part of verse 3 into verse 2, as a part of Micah's recital of what has already happened. We can understand the fear of Micah himself and his return of the silver, for money vowed to the Lord was under a taboo. Indeed, the curse may not have been so much in what the mother said as implicitly in the fact that what was taken was vowed to God. The curse could not be taken back, so the mother neutralized it with a blessing, and the restored silver was made into "a graven image and a molten image" by a silversmith. The duplication here may imply only one image, since "graven image" could be used in a general way and mean simply "idol." Micah apparently possessed a small shrine in which he housed this image along with an ephod and teraphim. The latter were small images. The ephod has already been discussed. It may have been either an image or a priestly vestment with pockets for the sacred dice used in oracular consultations. In any case this is not imageless worship. It may be that Micah worshiped the Lord in and through the images, or it may be that these were lesser and subservient deities associated with his family and his agricultural environment.

At this point, we see the attitude of the editor to the religious disorder of those days. Micah needed a priest for his shrine, so he appointed one of his sons to that office, an impossibility in the later days of the kingship when the priests formed a hereditary caste. The editor suggests that because there was no kingship in those days, every man acted according to his own light and within the pressure of tribal custom.

Micah's Levitical Priest (17:7-13)

Micah was apparently concerned to have a proper priest. The confusion of the times may be seen in the appointment of his son to priestly office, but apparently there was already a group of men, the Levites, who were regarded as specially fitted for the priestly function. The name Levite may, at this stage, refer rather to priestly status than to tribal origin, although the young man is specifically defined as a Judahite and historically the remnants of the Levites seem to have been absorbed within the tribe of Judah at the time of the Conquest. It may well be that these remnants early sought to perpetuate their tribal status by taking on priestly functions, although the term Levite seems to be more embracing than a mere tribal reference would suggest. Evidently others, like Micah's son, could be priests too, but the Levites were now making an exclusive bid for priestly office. Micah felt the necessity to have a priest who by training and background was able to consult the divine oracle efficiently and to direct the ritual of the shrine in proper manner. He naïvely believed that with such a Levite as his priest, God would favor him. The young man was offered the position of "father" as well as priest, but the word "father" here is an honorific title (vs. 10).

The Danite Spies at Micah's Shrine (18:1-6)

The writer of Judges once more reminds us that there was no king in Israel and consequently no central authority to guarantee law and order. Hence the Danites, subjected to pressures from the Amorites and possibly from Israelite neighbors, sought a place of permanent residence. They were resident in the south country just north of the area occupied by Judah, as the place names indicate. They sent out five spies to explore the land, and these men, as they moved into the hill country of Ephraim, came to the shrine of Micah, identified his Levite as a fellow countryman by his accent, and sought oracular guidance through him from God. The phrase "inquire of God" is a reminder that in these early days the priest's major task was to administer the traditional rules of the shrine and laws of the community and to consult the oracle for divine guidance upon the decisions and conduct of the worshipers. The chief method of divination seems to have been casting the sacred lots, two objects known tech-

nically as Urim and Thummim, by the falling of which the divine
guidance was ascertained. Alongside the priest there seems also
to have functioned quite early in the national and tribal shrines
the cultic prophet, who gave God's word through ecstatic vision
and oftentimes ecstatic utterance. Micah's was a private shrine,
however, and he had to be content with a priest instructed in the
art of divining God's will. The verdict was favorable in the case
of the spies, and they were told by the Levite to proceed in
peace, knowing that God was with them.

The Spies Find Laish (18:7-10)

The spies proceeded one hundred miles farther north and
came upon Laish. Near the sources of the River Jordan, this
city seems to have been colonized by people of Phoenician
origin. The spies were impressed by the security and wealth of
these inhabitants and by the fertility of the soil. Here was an easy
prey—a peaceful people living in a rich area. The spies returned
enthusiastically with the assurance that their people ought not to
miss this God-given opportunity. That they did regard this
as God-given implies a somewhat low and immoral view of the
divine will. The law that might is right and that the strong have
a right to dispossess the weak is a factor in the report of the spies.
There is no respect for the freedom of others. The Danites were
prepared to sacrifice this people's freedom and security for their
own. This is the law of the jungle. It is far removed from the
ethics of the Sermon on the Mount, and yet at this low and
material level it may prefigure the deeper, more spiritual, and
true conviction that God fights the spiritual battle for his people
and leads them into the wide open spaces of his love.

The Migration of the Danites (18:11-26)

The Danites sent six hundred men with wives and families
upon the northward migration (see vss. 11 and 21). The fact
that some Danites were still in the south in the Samson period
indicates that this group was not the whole tribe. They camped
at Kiriath-jearim and passed on into the hill country of Ephraim,
arriving at Micah's shrine. Here the spies told the migrants of the
sacred objects and oracle in the shrine. The Danites entered,
stole the images, kidnapped Micah's priest, and marched northward with their spoils. The priest seems to have been more or less
forcibly persuaded to accompany the migrants. Micah and his

neighbors pursued them and sought to recover his sacred objects and priest, but were threatened by the Danites and returned empty-handed, the thieves too strong for them.

The Capture of Laish (18:27-31)

The prosperous city of Laish was captured by the invaders. Its peaceful inhabitants, too far from Phoenicia to receive any help, were put to the sword, and its buildings were burned to the ground. The Danites raised a new city upon the site of the old, renamed it Dan, and founded a sanctuary within it. In this sanctuary they housed the sacred objects stolen from Micah and set his priest to serve the oracle. The shrine became one of the most famous in Israel, apparently claiming for its priesthood a direct descent from Moses and declaring it to be Levite. The text indicates that the name of Micah's Levite, who became the priest of Dan, was Jonathan and that he was the grandson of Moses (18:30). Thus the story, obviously early, is told to support the Danite claims.

The War with Benjamin (19:1—21:25)

The story in these chapters undoubtedly has a historical basis, but it also includes elements taken from folklore and traditions. The outrage at Gibeah may be hinted at in Hosea 9:9 and 10:9, and the story of the rape of the concubine has a vividness that savors of the early traditions recorded elsewhere in the Book of Judges. The extent of the destruction of the tribe of Benjamin in chapter 20 seems exaggerated, for it suggests almost a complete wiping out of the manpower of the tribe. The capture of virgins of Shiloh in chapter 21 reflects actual events. Since Saul came from Gibeah, it may be that this cycle of chapters was written against him and his tribe of Benjamin by those to whom his memory was odious. We have to remember that Jabesh-gilead was also associated with the Israelite king and owed him special gratitude (I Sam. 11:1-11; 31:11-13), a fact which would account for the somewhat extraneous inclusion of the sack of that city in chapter 21.

The Outrage of Gibeah (19:1-30)

In the days before the monarchy, a Levite of the hill country of Ephraim took a concubine from among the inhabitants of

Bethlehem. A quarrel followed, in consequence of which the woman returned to her father's home. The husband went after her, to "speak home to her heart," the literal meaning of the phrase "to speak kindly to her" (19:3). Accompanied by his servant and with two asses, he arrived at the father's house, was hospitably received, and was prevailed upon to prolong his stay. Reconciliation of the man and his concubine naturally called for feasting, and the latter was prolonged by the pressure of a father reluctant to let his daughter depart. At last, as night was falling on the fifth day, the Levite left for the return journey, with his concubine and his servant. They passed by Jebus, still a Canaanite city, more frequently referred to in the Bible by its other early name Jerusalem. The servant besought the Levite to stay here for the night, but he decided to pass on to Gibeah where the inhabitants were fellow Israelites. This city was later the home of Saul and was situated north of Jerusalem. As the party reached Gibeah, the sun set, and in that region the darkness would fall at once. Immediate lodging for the night was a necessity, but, despite their sitting in the market square where the social and business relationships were exercised, no one offered them hospitality. So inhospitable did Gibeah prove to be, despite the Levite's preferring it to Jebus with its Canaanite inhabitants, that ultimately it was an Ephraimite sojourner and not a resident of Gibeah who took them in.

As the Ephraimite sojourner entertained his guests, lewd fellows of Gibeah demanded that the Levite be sent out to them to satisfy their perverted sexuality. The remonstrances of the sojourner, who offered to send out his virgin daughter and the Levite's concubine, availed nothing. At last the Levite put out his concubine, who died of the outrages committed on her. The moral issue of the man substituting his concubine for himself was not an acute one in those early days, when women were regarded as man's possessions, not his equals and companions. We are apt to forget that the Hebrew world was a man's world and that women and children were understood to live entirely within the personal orbits of the men. The homosexuality of the lewd men of Gibeah was probably taken over from the Canaanites among whom it was practiced especially on festival occasions.

The Levite carried home the corpse of his concubine, and cut the body into twelve pieces, which he dispatched throughout the territory of Israel to stir up the Israelites because of the enormity

of the crime that had been committed. Saul later summoned the
Israelites to battle with the Ammonites by cutting up oxen and
sending the pieces to the tribes (I Sam. 11:6-7). Probably the
roots of the idea are related to magic; at any rate it was effective.
The closing verse is better rendered from the ancient Greek translation which reads that the Levite instructed the messengers who
carried the pieces of the body through Israel to say: "Did ever a
thing like this happen, from the day when the children of Israel
came up out of Egypt unto this day? Take counsel about it and
speak out."

The Punishment of Benjamin (20:1-48)

This chapter is much more complex than chapter 19. It exaggerates the situation. It is doubtful whether all Israel would be
involved in such an incident. It exaggerates the numbers participating and slain. The reference to the "congregation" of
Israel is usually regarded as an expression arising later in Israel's
history (see vs. 1). Yet there is certainly a historical core, whatever exaggerations may have been made of it, and we may be
sure that Benjamin was attacked and suffered severely and that
Gibeah was destroyed.

The Israelites gathered at Mizpah. The phrase "from Dan to
Beersheba" indicates that they came from the northern and
southern limits of the land; even Gilead across Jordan was included. Apparently, however, Jabesh-gilead refused to participate
(21:8). Mizpah was an ancient holy place situated in Benjamin.
The fact that it was in Benjamin might raise doubts as to whether
the assembly was made here. In any case, there was soon a move
to Bethel as center, as verses 18 and 26 make clear, and Mizpah
may be a later insertion. The Levite reported to the assembly the
crime against his concubine, implying that he thrust her out because they meant to kill him. That he could say this without apol-
ogy on his part or condemnation on the part of his hearers is again
a reminder that here we are dealing with a different and earlier
moral environment. Once more he appealed for counsel. The in-
dignation of the hearers was such that they unanimously committed themselves to an immediate punitive expedition against Gibeah. They devised a method whereby it should be provisioned by
those of their number chosen by lot.

Before advancing, the Israelite band sent an ultimatum to the
tribe of Benjamin, demanding that the lewd criminals be given to

them for execution. The execution of these "base fellows" was
declared to be the way of putting away the evil from Israel.
Atonement, in other words, demanded the punishment of the
criminals. We need to remember the part played in the early Hebrew mind by the sense of social solidarity. The crime of the men
of Gibeah had exposed all Israel to punishment, and the guilt
resting on all Israel could be removed only when these men were
wiped out. We have a similar situation in the story of Achan
(Joshua 7:20-26). It appears again in the story of the men of
Gibeon (II Sam. 21). The Benjaminites refused to surrender
the culprits, and war was joined.

The Benjaminites were expert archers and slingers (see I Chron.
12:2-7), with the result that the Israelite host had to face two
successive defeats before it had the situation in hand. The numbers involved on both sides are evidently exaggerated, and it is
probable that verses 37-44 give a more sober estimate of the
forces involved.

The center of operations was Bethel. Here, before beginning
battle, Israelites went to consult the oracle. If we judge by the
questions asked (vss. 23 and 27), which could have a "yes" or
"no" answer, the method used must have been that of the sacred
lot. Judah led the first attack against Gibeah, under divine instruction. The Israelites were defeated, many being killed by the superior stone-slinging of their foes. Distressed, they once more
sought oracular advice and again were directed to attack, only to
suffer defeat again. Fasting and making burnt offerings, they yet
a third time sought oracular guidance from God. We are told that
the Ark was at Bethel at this time, apparently having been moved
from Shiloh, and also that the Aaronite priest Phinehas ministered
before it. This Phinehas has been identified as the predecessor of
Eli. The fact that he supported the punitive expedition probably
explains the stubborn persistence of the Israelite hosts despite successive defeats. The third consultation of the divine oracle
brought the assurance of triumph. This time the Israelites en-
trapped the Benjaminites by dissembling flight, drawing their foes
away from the city defenses of Gibeah onto the highways, and
there ambushing them. A great slaughter of the men of Benjamin
ensued. The ruse employed is similar to that used by the Israelites
before Ai (Joshua 8:14-17).

In verses 37-44, we come upon evidence of the complex structure of this chapter. Evidently this is a second account of the final

defeat of the Benjaminites and the sack of Gibeah. This story is more realistic than the other and may well be nearer to the actual events. The Israelites in ambush, according to this account, fell upon Gibeah and sent it up in flames, once the Benjaminites had been lured out of it. The latter, at the sight of the city going up in smoke behind them, fled in dismay to the eastern hills or wilderness, and were slain in great numbers as they fled. The closing verses of this section probably give, as we have suggested, a more realistic account of the numbers involved. Only six hundred men of Benjamin were left alive, and they took refuge at the rock of Rimmon.

The Fate of Benjamin and the Rape of Shiloh (21:1-25)

At Mizpah the other tribes had taken an oath to abstain from intermarriage of their daughters with the men of Benjamin. But so great had been the slaughter of the Benjaminites that the conscience of Israel was troubled. The six hundred men remaining to Benjamin had to be provided with wives if that tribe was not to face extinction, yet the Israelites must keep their oath. They gathered before the Lord at Bethel, with misgiving and concern, seeking a way out of the impasse. Then they remembered that those who did not join their expedition against Benjamin were under curse of death, and they recalled that the men of Jabesh-gilead had held back. They sent a detachment of their host to destroy the inhabitants, saving only the virgins. By this exploit, they found four hundred brides for the remnant of the Benjaminites. They returned with these, not to Bethel, but to Shiloh, whither apparently the Israelite camp had been transferred. There the Benjaminites were summoned from the rock of Rimmon and given their brides, but the brides were not sufficient in number.

With compassion still in their hearts and desiring to heal the breach in their tribal confederacy, the Israelites sought for yet more brides. The burden of their oath still rested on them, however, so they still had to supply the need circuitously. An annual festival to the Lord was due at Shiloh; it appears to have been at the vintage harvest, and during it the daughters of Shiloh danced around the vineyards. The Benjaminites were told to be in wait, and to seize each man a wife from among the dancing maidens. The Israelites argued that in this way they could get around the oath taken at Mizpah, for the Shilonites would not have given these women to the Benjaminites as wives. They would be taken without the previous consent of their fathers. Furthermore, a feud or vendetta between Shiloh and the Benjaminites would be avoided, since the maidens would not have been taken in battle or with loss of life. Hence the leaders of Israel planned to plead with their fellow Israelites from Shiloh that they graciously permit their daughters to remain with the Benjaminites. The plan was carried out successfully, and the tribe of Benjamin was saved from extinction.

THE BOOK OF
RUTH

INTRODUCTION

This short book occurs in the third section of the Hebrew Old Testament, the section entitled "the Writings." It was transferred to its present position in the Greek Version and is actually where it belongs, for it reflects in content the period of the judges. It is a story which describes faithfully many of the conditions and customs of those early days, even though the writing in its present form was probably quite late, possibly after the Exile, and even perhaps after Nehemiah and Ezra, in the fourth century B.C. The lateness of the writing is indicated by the fact that the writer was evidently familiar with the Book of Judges in its final form (Ruth 1:1). Furthermore, the author can describe a custom in 4:7 as no longer practiced. Finally, some of the style and language may belong to a much later period than that of the story. Yet the writer has been careful to preserve the customs and atmosphere of those far-off days and was familiar with traditions that had been faithfully preserved from antiquity.

The story is interesting for the light it throws on levirate marriage, according to which a brother-in-law should marry his brother's widow and raise up children to his dead brother. The story moves beyond the brother relationship, for Boaz was not a brother but only a kinsman of the deceased sons of Naomi. The late time of recording the story may be reflected in the refusal of one kinsman to accept the responsibility because it would impair his own inheritance.

The implication is that monogamy was the accepted practice, but this was not true in the time of the judges. The Deuteronomic form of the law makes it clear that a man may marry his brother's widow even though he is already married. This marriage with the brother's widow would not impair the inheritance of any children that he had by the wife to whom he was already wed. It is the latter children who carry on his own family and extend his name (Deut. 25:5-10).

Some suggest that the story may be an apologetic in favor of foreign marriages at a time when these were being attacked. We immediately call to mind the days of Nehemiah and Ezra when there was some attempt to keep Judaism pure by banning any marriage alliances with aliens. Actually, however, Ruth had accepted her mother-in-law's faith and customs before she approached Boaz, and thus could rank as a proselyte. Proselytes were never excluded from marriage alliances with natural-born Jews, therefore the idea that the book is a polemic falls to the ground. Moreover, it does not breathe a polemic atmosphere. We may assume that it was written to preserve a tradition that David's royal line had Moabite blood in its veins, and to emphasize the true universalism of Israel's faith, in which even a Moabitess could share and share significantly. It remained for great David's "greater Son" to open the Kingdom to all believers and show that all men, no matter what their race or color, could share in the blessings of the People of God.

OUTLINE

COMMENTARY

THREE WIDOWS IN MOAB

Ruth 1:1-18

Sometime during the period covered by the Book of Judges, a famine in Palestine caused a Hebrew family to migrate from Bethlehem in Judah, David's birthplace, to Moab. Other references to such famines in Palestine are found in Genesis 12:10; 26:1; 41:56; II Samuel 21:1; and I Kings 17. The name "Elimelech" is compounded of the words for "God" and "king" and means "God is King." The name of Elimelech's wife means "pleasant" or "agreeable." Elimelech died, and the sons married Moabite wives, Orpah and Ruth.

When the sons died also, Naomi determined to return to the homeland, having received information that the famine had ceased. She was accompanied by her two daughters-in-law, who thus turned their backs on their native land and on memories of a happy married life. She appears to have been aggressive in leadership, but her determination was blended with tenderness and sympathy. She sought to persuade the other two women to return to their homes and remain in Moab. Although Ruth, at least, had a father living (2:11), she was bidden to return to her mother's home. The daughter's place was in the mother's tent, for this was the Bedouin practice. The reference is to the women's quarters required in polygamous marriage.

Ruth and Orpah persisted in desiring to go with Naomi, and once more she pleaded with them to return home. She had no more sons to give them as husbands, and she was too old to bear any. Moreover, any future child of hers would in any case be too young for her daughters-in-law. Behind her plea lies the thought of the law of levirate marriage, according to which if a man died without issue, his brother should take the widow to wife and raise up a son to the dead brother (Deut. 25:5-6). The custom was widespread in the ancient Near East, but in Naomi's case age made its effectiveness questionable. In the story of Judah and Tamar we have an instance of a daughter-in-law waiting in seclusion for another son to reach marriageable age and perform the levirate obligation (Gen. 38:11), but Naomi did not want her daughters secluded too long. Moreover, she saw God's hand in her tragedy and was prepared to accept it with resignation.

Orpah decided to return, but Ruth still clung to her mother-in-law. Naomi sought to dissuade her in an argument which stressed the current belief that in leaving her homeland Ruth was also leaving her god, since the deity and the land were so tied together that the deity had no jurisdiction outside the country. This is an indication of the primitive level of religion at this stage. Ruth refused to be put off. With a fine exhibition of personal devotion, she declared herself ready to forsake her Moabite heritage, to accept the people and the God of Naomi, and, for Naomi's sake, to live her life out in a foreign land. Her words enshrine the noblest expression of friendship. We note that at the end of Ruth's speech she is represented as using the familiar Hebrew name for God ("Yahweh," rendered "LORD" in the Revised Standard Version). Even a Moabitess and a foreigner might trust in him and follow him.

THE ARRIVAL IN BETHLEHEM
Ruth 1:19-22

Naomi and Ruth continued on their way to Bethlehem, where their arrival created a great stir (the Hebrew word here literally means "a buzz of conversation"). We can imagine the rumors that were rife and the ill-natured gossip, for had Naomi not forsaken the Lord and gone to the land of Chemosh, the god of the Moabites? Naomi declared herself to be afflicted of God and bade them call her Mara, or "bitter." She had gone away a happy woman with a husband and two boys, and she was returning empty.

RUTH THE GLEANER
Ruth 2:1-23

At this point Boaz is introduced as a wealthy man and as belonging to the same family tree as Naomi's dead husband, Elimelech. Ruth now became the family supporter and sought for some livelihood by gleaning after the reapers in the harvest field. An old custom, legalized in the law code of Deuteronomy (24: 19-21), permitted the needy stranger, orphan, or widow to gather what was left by the harvesters. In its legal form, indeed, the injunction implied that the field should not be swept clean but that some should be left. Even so, we can imagine that often little was left, and gleaning might be a thankless task in the heat of the day. It was not made easier for a young foreign woman like Ruth, who might be molested by the laborers.

Ruth gleaned by chance in the part of the field owned by Boaz, although the story shows that, as so often happens in the life of the pious, it was not chance at work but the hand of God. Boaz, coming from Bethlehem, saluted his reapers with a pious greeting which shows the quality of his character, a greeting similar to that used by the angel to Gideon (Judges 6:12) and still employed in Christian liturgies.

Impressed by the appearance of the young stranger, Boaz learned that she was the Moabitess who had returned with Naomi, and who had been industriously gleaning after the reapers since early morning. Boaz gave her special privileges and provided for her safety, since the laborers might be crude in their conduct. He put her with his maidens who gathered the sheaves, and he warned the young men against molesting her. He also provided for her physical needs. Ruth humbly acknowledged his favor, emphasizing by a play on words the fact that she was an alien. (The Hebrew words for "foreigner" and "to take notice of" have the same root.) Boaz apparently knew the story of Ruth's devotion to her mother-in-law, a devotion that had led her to forsake her own kith and kin. His invocation of the divine blessing upon her acknowledged that she had now put her trust in the God of Israel, and was sheltering under his wing or skirt. Ruth expressed grateful surprise that she, a foreigner, should be so treated (2:10, 13). The favor continued at mealtime, for Boaz continued to treat her as if she were an Israelite by making her share in the food.

Because of this gracious treatment Ruth gleaned long and well, returned amply supplied, and shared her leftover food with Naomi. On informing Naomi that she had gleaned in the field of Boaz, Ruth learned that he was a kinsman. Naomi added that Boaz was one of their nearest kin, showing that she was beginning to evaluate the interest of the wealthy farmer and that her mind was turning to the levirate law of the kinsman-redeemer which Boaz later invoked. This is probably implied in Naomi's blessing upon Boaz, who by his kindness showed that God had not forsaken either the living or the dead. Boaz must accept responsibility for the widowed and childless Ruth. He must be her redeemer.

RUTH FINDS A REDEEMER
Ruth 3:1-18

As Naomi saw it, the kinsman-redeemer needed to be awakened
to his responsibility, so she laid her plans for doing this. When
the barley was being winnowed and the harvest was almost over,
license often prevailed. The harvest had been associated by the
ancient peoples of Palestine with fertility rites, and even the Hebrews had accepted some of these practices and customs, while
hypothetically retaining their wilderness religion. There is evidence of this in Judges. The winnowing took place in the evening
hours when a cool breeze blew in from the Mediterranean Sea,
and the workers slept on the threshing floor to protect the grain.
Ruth was instructed by Naomi to prepare herself as a bride, wait
until Boaz had eaten and drunk, and then, as he slept, to uncover
his feet and lie there. She did as instructed, and at midnight Boaz
awoke to find the woman at his feet. In the darkness, she identified
herself and pleaded that he spread his skirt over her, since he was
her next of kin. This act of covering with the skirt was a familiar
one in the ancient Near East and was symbolic of protection; it
was especially associated with marriage. We note that just as
Boaz in his prayer had described Ruth as taking refuge under the
wings or skirts of the Lord, so now a like refuge was requested of
him. Boaz accepted his responsibility, emphasizing that Ruth's devotion and Covenant love ("first" kindness) to Naomi were now
matched by a greater devotion and Covenant love ("last" kindness) to himself (vs. 10). He kept her in safety for the rest of
the night, promising that the next day he would set in process his
active role as kinsman. He reminded her that there was one other
nearer kinsman on whom the priority in the duty rested.

Boaz vowed that if this man failed, he himself would marry
Ruth the next morning. Ruth returned to Naomi before daybreak,
Boaz having instructed his servants that her presence on the
threshing floor must be kept secret. Boaz sealed his vow with a
gift of barley, and Ruth came back to Naomi with reassuring
news.

BOAZ REDEEMS RUTH
Ruth 4:1-12

Boaz now proceeded with his purpose. All village business of importance was decided at the gate, where the elders of the community gave advice and judgment. Boaz selected ten men to apply their wisdom to his problem and act as witnesses to his impending transaction. The Hebrew at this point seems to indicate that Naomi had already disposed of her dead husband's property. Questions have been raised as to when she did so and how she as a widow could even own property under Hebrew law (see Num. 27:8-11), but both Hebrew law and practice are too conflicting at this point for us to make a judgment. It is clear, however, that part of the levirate law consisted in the injunction that the next of kin should redeem by purchase the family lands (Lev. 25:25). In the formulation of the law in Leviticus, which is late, the next of kin is identified with the brother of the deceased man, but we may assume that the range of kinship was wider in earlier times. It certainly appears to have been so in this story, for neither Boaz nor the nearest of kin was a brother of Elimelech's son, Ruth's husband. Boaz, however, challenged the nearest of kin to redeem Naomi's property. Ruth, as an alien, could not inherit her husband's property. Boaz was careful to point out that whoever redeemed the land must also marry Ruth the Moabitess, the widow of the dead son, in order to raise up seed to the dead. Boaz used the expression "buy" to express this latter act, but Ruth could not be bought, for she was no one's property, and it seems best to assume that the storyteller means simply that buying the land carried with it obligations with regard to Ruth. It was implied in such a levirate marriage that the first-born son of the marriage should rank as the son of the dead man and not be legally his father's son. Hence the nearest kin could hold that this would impair his own inheritance. He was unwilling to build up the house of his kinsman. Boaz, of course, was willing, so the next of kin took off his shoe as a sign that he renounced his right. Again the practice varied, for according to Deuteronomy 25:9 the widow loosed the shoe of the unwilling party and spat in his face, but the Book of Ruth represents days when such practices were varied and a norm had not yet been established.

Boaz proceeded to play the role of kinsman-redeemer. It is significant that this term should later be applied to God's relation to his people Israel (Isa. 41:14; 43:14; 44:6). Boaz purchased the land in the presence of the ten witnessing elders and took Ruth to wife to perpetuate the name of the dead. The community expressed good wishes to Boaz, assuming that more than one son would be born of the union and that the house of Boaz, as well as that of the dead, would be built up. Tamar, like Ruth, was a childless widow, and her case may have been cited both because she bore twins and as a delicate compliment to Ruth.

THE MARRIAGE AND ITS CONSEQUENCES
Ruth 4:13-22

A son was born to Boaz and Ruth through whom the name of Elimelech was perpetuated, so that it could be said that a son was born to Naomi through the selfless devotion of Ruth and the equally unselfish attitude of Boaz. Naomi's taking the child to her breast was a sign of acceptance. The child was named Obed.

There is in this story a striking illustration of how God raises the humble and uses the weak things of the world for his glory. Ruth, the childless widow and Moabitess, an alien so far as the People of God were concerned, became, in God's purpose, the progenitor of the Davidic line and the ancestress of him who was to be the Messiah, through whom God would deliver his people and rebuild them from among all nations. Closely bound up with this is the theme that one born outside Israel's Covenant could yet share in that Covenant and be a partaker of the faith.

The verb "to redeem"—"to act the part of kinsman"—which is applied to the selfless Boaz is used in Isaiah and Job to describe God's activity (Isa. 43:1, 14; 44:22; 47:4; 48:17; 49:7; 52:9; Job 19:25). Further, such redemptive activity of God comes to historical focus in the Person of Jesus Christ, the descendant in his humanity of the man who redeemed Ruth and Naomi.

The concluding genealogical table is generally regarded as a later addition to the original story. According to the story, the child was to be reckoned in the line of Elimelech, and not that of Boaz as in verses 18-22. Probably the priestly editors of Hebrew history, who were particularly fond of genealogies, were anxious to emphasize David's Judean descent.

THE FIRST AND SECOND BOOKS OF

SAMUEL

INTRODUCTION

The Character of the Books

A reading of the Books of Samuel shows that they are the same type of literature as that found in the Book of Judges. The same motifs are to be found—the emphasis on divine retribution for sin at the personal and national levels, the concern with the centrality of the prophetic consciousness in Israel's history. There are also the first signs of a new motif—the Temple at Jerusalem as the focal point of Israel's life. It is true that the account of the building of the Temple comes in the Books of Kings, but here we have the story of the conquest of Jerusalem, the account of David's sudden and conscience-prodded desire to build a house for the Lord, and the record of the historical vicissitudes of the Ark of the Lord in its progress toward its final resting place in the Temple at Jerusalem. The books are valuable to us for the insights they offer into the nature of the prophetic consciousness, into the ministry of the priests and the practice of oracular divination, into the nature of the sacrificial system, into the importance of the Ark in Israel's worship, into the democratic nature of the kingship, and into the Covenantal structure of Israel's society.

As in the case of the Book of Judges, the present form of the Books of Samuel is the work of an editor or editors who share the prophetic view of history found in the Book of Deuteronomy. They have made use of a considerable amount of earlier material, most of it probably written down by the time it reached them. Because there were often two versions of the same event available, we shall find that, in the Books of Samuel, different accounts will be given in succession.

Part of the task of the historian is to gather the historical truth from both accounts and weigh the actual historical happening. Yet we have to remember once more that the Bible is not a purely historical record and that the writers were not concerned with details, variations in which may disturb us. Their main emphasis was on what the living God was saying in history, and they were interested in events at the level of revelation. Hence they are prepared to offer varying versions of the same event, so long as the revelation stands clear.

Sources

We shall now enumerate some of the earlier sources used by the editors. The Books of Samuel fall into three main sections. The first part, I Samuel 1-12, deals with the story of Samuel; the second part, I Samuel 13-31, covers the history of Saul; the third part, II Samuel, presents the story of David. Within the third part, II Samuel 9-20 seems to depend upon a contemporary source, which may be thought of as the "Court History of David." It is characterized by a faithful portrayal of the Israelite king, with no attempt to cover up the blemishes in his character, his moral lapses, and his errors in judgment, or to evade recording his troubles. Thus David's adultery with Bathsheba is told with acknowledgment of his guilt, while the rebellion of Absalom is recorded in a way that conveys a sense of reality. These "court annals" are generally accepted as dating back to David's time.

The early chapters of Samuel seem to draw on a source preserving traditions of the prophet's childhood, and on one dealing with the history of the Ark. Possibly the latter source is also used in II Samuel 6 and 7, where we are told of the movement of the Ark to Jerusalem and of David's desire to build a temple, although these chapters may have been taken from the Temple records.

It is when we come to the stories of Saul and of the early years of David that we meet duplicate versions of the same event. There are two accounts of how Saul became king (I Sam. 8; 10:17-27; and 9:1—10:16; ch. 11). In the first account Israel's desire for a king is regarded as a defection from God's sole kingship; Samuel anoints Saul but also gives a warning of what Israel may expect from an earthly monarch. The other account associates Saul's kingship with God's express choice through his prophet, and this regards the monarchy as a divinely ordained institution under God's blessing. There are also two accounts of David's flight to Achish (I Sam. 21:10-15 and 27:1-12), two versions of his sparing Saul (I Sam. 24:1-22 and 26:1-25), and two descriptions of Saul's death (I Sam. 31:1-7 and II Sam. 1:1-16). There are also two accounts of how David became associated with Saul, one picturing David as a shepherd boy and the other presenting him as a musician and armor-bearer. These are discussed in the commentary. At this point, it is sufficient to note that the editors seem to have been using two sources dealing with Saul's kingship and David's early years. The earlier source regarded the institution of kingship favorably and presented it as under God's blessing. The later source described the kingship as an act of apostasy in which the people had turned to an earthly leader rather than relying on God. It reflects the attitude toward the monarchy shown in Hosea 10:9 and possibly also the attitude of the editors themselves. We may say that the first source was much more nearly contemporaneous with the events it records, and that the second was later and shows the attitude toward the monarchy which developed after some experience of it. It would be wrong, however, to regard this second source as less significant, since it may well reflect an attitude that went back to the early days of the monarchy, although then less in evidence. It may also preserve genuine traditions and details that amplify the earlier source.

The Books of Samuel contain many interesting poetic fragments—the song of Hannah (I Sam. 2:1-10); the lament of David over Saul and Jonathan (II Sam. 1:19-27); the lament of David over Abner (II Sam. 3:33-34); David's hymn of thanksgiving (II Sam. 22); and the testament of David (II Sam. 23:1-7). Of these, it is generally agreed that the song of Hannah does not strictly describe Hannah's experience, and probably was written later. The hymn of thanksgiving ascribed to David also occurs as Psalm 18. In its present form it was probably written after David's time. There is no reason why the two laments should not be the actual compositions of David, and we may also ascribe to him the testament of II Samuel 23:1-7, even though it does not reach the poetic heights of the laments and presents a somewhat idealized picture. These psalms and the representation of David as a musician remind us that the tradition enshrined in the Book of Psalms, which made David the psalmist of Israel par excellence, had some foundation in the events of David's own life.

A miscellaneous appendix is added to the Books of Samuel (II Sam. 21—24), in which the editors have gathered various pieces of tradition and reports which could not be fitted into the main body of the history writing.

OUTLINE

COMMENTARY

SAMUEL, JUDGE AND PROPHET
I Samuel 1:1—8:22

Samuel's Early Years (1:1—3:21)

The Birth of Samuel (1:1—2:10)

Samuel's parentage indicates that he was of Ephraimite stock and that his mother was one of two wives. The practice of bigamy seems to have been widespread in these early days, chiefly because of fear that there would be no offspring (see the comment on Judges 11:34-40).

The family of Samuel was deeply religious, and attended annually the sanctuary at Shiloh, probably immediately after harvest, to offer thanks in the form of sacrifice for the Lord's blessing. Although the visit may have been associated with some annual festival, it was apparently a private one and was linked with a vow (vs. 21). The sacrifice was a corporate family act, with the wives and family participating with Elkanah in the presentation of gifts. In verse 3 the title "the LORD of hosts" is used of God for the first time in Old Testament literature. It is usually assumed to be a reference to the armies of Israel rather than to the host of heavenly bodies, since the noun "host" when used for the latter is only in the singular. The title is indeed in keeping with the concept of the "holy war" which dominated this period, and in which the Lord was regarded as the war leader of his people. In I Samuel 17:45, we have an actual definition in these terms: "the LORD of hosts, the God of the armies of Israel." Later usage simply took over the title as a proper name for God with little or no remembrance of the original significance.

Eli the priest, with his two sons, is introduced somewhat abruptly. We know little about this priestly family and it soon dropped out of religious history, but the distinction of ministering at the important shrine of Shiloh is indicative of Eli's standing. Hannah, the favorite wife of Elkanah, had no children. Taunted by her rival, Hannah seized the opportunity of the visit to Shiloh to express to the Lord her own private needs. She prayed for a

child and made her vows. Her agitated behavior conveyed to Eli
the impression of drunkenness, a condition not unknown in those
early shrines, when naturalistic ideas and fertility-rite practices
were often present in the religious consciousness of the ordinary
worshiper. She apparently added to this impression by the fact
that she prayed in her heart, that is, prayed silently; normally
prayer was made aloud, and the movement of her lips was misin-
terpreted. Rebuked by the old priest, Hannah laid bare her problem and received his sympathy and encouragement. The vow she
made was that the child should be dedicated wholly to the service
of God, and that he should go with head unshaven all of his life.
The law that everything which first opens the womb belongs to
God and has to be redeemed appears to make this vow unnecessary, although it has been suggested that Hannah's vow implies
that she did not intend to exercise the right of redemption.

In due time the promise was fulfilled. Hannah bore a son
whom she named Samuel, which means "name of God." The relation of this name to the explanation "asked . . . of the LORD"
(vs. 20), actually descriptive of the name Saul, has caused considerable perplexity and remains a matter of speculation.

Once more the time for the annual visit arrived, but Hannah
refrained from participation until the child had been weaned. At
that time the vow was fulfilled, and Samuel was returned perma-
nently to God who had given him. With him, Samuel's parents
presented provisions for his sustenance, bullocks, meal, and wine.
His mother also kept him in clothing (2:19).

A break in the narrative comes in 2:1-10, indicating the multi-
plicity of sources and traditions on which the Hebrew historians
drew. The song of Hannah in these verses is manifestly quite
early, but in its present form it seems to be a national song cele-
brating the triumph of a king in battle (vs. 10). The reference to
a "king" dates it later than Hannah since it was not until after her
time that a king came to the throne of Israel. It celebrates God's
providence and speaks of God as the special friend of the poor,
the humble, and the needy. The reference to the barren who bears
seven (vs. 5) may well have been the occasion for the association
of Hannah with the psalm, although it has a different setting from
her special need. The exaltation of the meek and the striking
down of the mighty find a worthy echo in the Magnificat (Luke
1:46-55), whose author seems consciously to have had this psalm
as a model.

Certain phrases need to be noted. First, there are expressions like "my strength is exalted," literally, "my horn is exalted," and "my mouth derides," literally, "my mouth is enlarged" (2:1). The first expression is a poetic reference to the animal which lifts up its horned head in triumph, sure of its power. The second expression carries the memory that a gaping mouth was, for the Hebrew, a sign of contempt.

Secondly, the emphasis on God's holiness carries with it the sense of his uniqueness and otherness. There is none beside him, and he is especially marked by his rocklike stability. For the Hebrew this holiness of God signifies God's character, and since he is the living God, his holiness is a dynamic quality. It does not mean a withdrawn otherness. Holiness is an otherness of God that is also manifested in his action within Israel's history. He is a source of strength to his people, and the psalmist sees this as the exaltation of the weak and the bringing down of the mighty in battle (vs. 4). Because of his utter dependence on God's holy power, a man may not boast of his exploits (vs. 3), an insight which in the New Testament is brought out in Paul's condemnation of justification by works.

Thirdly, the primitive view of the world appears in the suggestion that God has set the world on "the pillars of the earth" (vs. 8). This is a reference to the Hebrew picture of the universe as set upon pillars in the midst of the deep, the primordial sea which embraces the disclike earth and domelike heaven.

Fourthly, we find an emphasis on the deliverance of God's people. The adversaries of God will be broken in pieces, but "his faithful ones," the saints, will be delivered (vs. 9). The word is derived from the same root as the word translated "loving kindness," or "covenant love." It is a covenant word, emphasizing the steadfast loyalty to one another to which the parties of a covenant are mutually bound. So God is bound to his Covenant people, and his faithful ones are those who respond to his steadfast loyalty with a corresponding faithfulness in the Covenant. True piety is manifested in loyalty and steadfastness, and for such as manifest it, God's Covenant love never fails. It is interesting to note that in the Book of Psalms, the same term has become a technical description of the pious Jew, who is often identified with the poor, the oppressed, and the humble, an idea also present in this poem.

Fifthly, the reference to the king as the "anointed" (vs. 10), the Messiah, may point to the ideal king yet to come. Yet every

Davidic king was regarded as "anointed," and the psalm may refer to the actual monarchy. This certainly dates the psalm in the time of the monarchy, and thus much later than Hannah.

Eli's Sons and Samuel (2:11-36)

The sons of Eli are described as worthless men who knew not the Lord. The term "have regard" here, and in the Old Testament generally, although sometimes translated "know," refers to a personal encounter in which God meets us directly and confronts us with his will. Thus it is synonymous with personal commitment. It means more than awareness that God exists, or having some speculative idea of God in the mind. The latter is more in keeping with the Greek understanding of knowledge. The Old Testament term means living decisively within the Covenant which God has established; seeking to do his will; walking before him in faithfulness, obedience, and humility.

The condemnation of Eli's sons is based also on their practice in the sanctuary. The phrase "custom of the priests" suggests a precedent established by long practice and thus regarded as binding. The law books of the Pentateuch contain many such customs which were regarded as given under divine authority. We need to remember that God has various ways of manifesting his moral law to men, and that one way is through the development of habitual lines of conduct within the give-and-take of social relationship and the commerce of wills. So here the shrine at Shiloh had developed certain rules with regard to the ordering of its sacrifices, and these rules were regarded as morally binding upon priest and worshiper. They were ritual rules with moral implications because they were under divine sanction. The sacrifices were offered to God, and thus the rules governing them were under his authority. The worshiper or priest who broke the rules would be treating God with contempt.

The crime of Eli's sons was that they took for their own use parts of the sacrifice other than that which was their rightful due. As the law codes developed, there seems to have been a universal ruling on this matter (Deut. 18:3; Lev. 7:31-34), but, even at this early stage, Phinehas and Hophni were familiar with the rule for their own shrine and contravened it. Their crime was twofold. They claimed their meat raw instead of taking it from the boiling pot by a three-toothed fork. But, further, they claimed it prior to the burning of the fat. To understand this we have to remember that the sacrifice here thought of was the "peace" or communion meal offering. In this type of sacrifice, the beast was slain; the blood, as the element containing the life principle, was drained off and poured out at the foot of the altar; the fat and entrails were burned up on the altar; and the remaining flesh was eaten by the worshipers, the priests claiming their part. Until the fat had been burned, the sacrifice was totally holy; it was available to the worshiper only after the burning. The terrible crime of Eli's sons was that they disregarded the holiness of the sacrifice and claimed their portion before it had become profane or available for human participation.

In God's eyes the sacrifice thereby became abhorrent. Its end was not to give God glory but to satisfy gluttonous priests. Are not many of our more modern sacrifices tainted in a similar way?

Samuel is described in verse 18 as wearing an ephod, here clearly not an image but a priestly garment (see Judges 17:5). This is one of the enigmatic words of the Old Testament, the usage of which may have changed in the course of Israel's history and may have varied locally from shrine to shrine. Samuel's mother still kept the boy clothed, and the annual visit of his family to the sanctuary continued.

In his indictment of Eli's sons, the historian now adds to their crime of gluttonous disregard of sacrificial rules the sin of adultery (vss. 22-25). The reference to "the tent of meeting" may indicate that prior to the erection of the sanctuary at Shiloh, there was a sacred tent to house the Ark of the Covenant and that this still existed. Be that as it may, the sins were serious enough, and their full significance is drawn out in verse 25—they were sins against the Lord directly. In the Hebrew mind, God would be more concerned here than in the case of a crime between man and man. In the case of Eli's sons there was no one to intercede, for God himself was offended and vengeance must descend from heaven. We miss the emphasis that even to sin against one's fellow men is to sin against God. The distinction introduced here into the problem of moral evil finds no parallel in the full development of the biblical revelation. God's inevitable judgment is clearly implied by Eli, and the historian declares that it was the will of the Lord to slay Eli's sons. We need, at this point, to remember that the devout Hebrew, unlike the speculative Greek, had no interest in intermediary causes. For the Hebrew, God is active in, with, and under all nature and history. Thus the processes of history or nature were not the final causes of events in the created order. God was the final cause, and his judgments as well as his saving activity directed and sustained natural and historical processes, working in accord with natural and moral law, in which they were fulfilled. Thus the historical processes might bring about the deaths of Hophni and Phinehas, but it could be said that the Lord would slay them.

Verses 27-36 form an editorial addition, concerned to explain the replacement of Eli's family in the priesthood by the Zadokite group of priests. The actual supersedure is recorded in I Kings 2:27, where we are told that Solomon ousted Abiathar from being priest in fulfillment of the prophetic word spoken at Shiloh. This story is significant as introducing an authentic prophet who declares the doom of Eli's house. The prophetic oracle links Eli with the house of Aaron; the only evidence for this would be the usage of the Aaronic family name, Phinehas, for Eli's son.

The prophet declared that the crime of Eli's sons would surely lead to the divine judgment. The implied references in verses 33-34 are various. Verse 33 probably refers to the massacre of the priests at Nob from which Abiathar alone survived (22:18, 20). Verse 34 probably has a double reference to the death of Eli's sons, Hophni and Phinehas, in battle, and also to the final ousting of Abiathar in the time of Solomon. The mention of "a faithful priest" who should be raised up in the place of this corrupt priesthood (vs. 35) would then be a reference to Zadok, but it might also refer to Samuel. We need to remember that though a prophetic word was spoken to a contemporary historical situation, the principles enunciated in it and the prophetic insight into the divine will meant that its fulfillment might be extended down history and be manifested in more than one event. Apparently this passage was written down long after the unknown prophet gave his oracle; but looking back along the stream of events, the historian saw the outcome of that oracle of judgment in successive incidents such as those in the battle with the Philistines, in the affair at Nob, and in the fall of Abiathar.

The Call of Samuel (3:1-21)

This familiar story is a reminder of how God often works in history. Weak leadership by an old man, whose worthless sons were using the priestly office for their own ends, had brought the people to the verge of disaster. The opening verse of this chapter expresses this situation in the declaration that the word of God, the prophetic oracle, was "rare." Authentic insight into God's counsels, such as he gave to his genuine prophets, had become a rare occurrence, and therefore was greatly treasured. At such a moment God acts to raise the man for the hour, and often it is the weak and lowly who are so exalted in order that the power may manifestly be God's and not man's.

Samuel's task was apparently to serve as attendant to the Ark, near which he slept in the Temple. The Ark itself has been a matter of considerable debate. It is described as a rectangular box, with two poles attached for transportation, containing, according to tradition, the two tablets of the Law (Exod. 25 and 37). The lid of the box was termed "the mercy seat," and two cherubim, possibly early representations of angels, were set above this lid. The Ark was the center of God's presence among his people. It was his throne, and here he dwelt in the midst of his people (Exod. 25:8-22). Thus to come before the Ark meant to come before the Lord, and to take the Ark to battle meant that God himself would come among his people and save them from their enemies (I Sam. 4:4). When the Ark was lifted and moved forward before the people in their wilderness wanderings, it was equivalent to God's arising that his enemies might flee before him (Num. 10:35-36). Thus we may say that the Ark was a tangible sign of God's presence among his people. It brought the divine presence to a focus and could be described as his "throne." As the Ark was in some sense an extension of God's personal being into the visible realm, it was to a degree an anticipation of the Incarnation. Of the Ark it could be said, "Immanuel"—"God with us."

Since messages from God were infrequent in those days, we can understand Eli's reaction to the experiences of Samuel recorded in 3:1-9. By its threefold repetition the experience was proved to be real and not hallucinatory, and Eli was convinced that Samuel was being called by the Lord himself. Samuel, whose training hitherto had been for the priesthood, was now called of God to be a prophet, and the content of his first prophetic message was disclosed to him—the divine judgment on Eli's house. This inaugural vision or audition initiated Samuel into both the reality of the Hebrew faith and his prophetic task. Like the other prophetic figures of Israel, Samuel had an initiatory experience in which the burden of his message was made plain. Eli's greatness

is disclosed in his recognition that God was working out his purpose in Samuel's life, and still more so in his resigned acceptance
of the prophetic message when his young attendant declared it to
him. The sin of Eli's house had become so deep that sacrifice
would not avail to cover it and final destruction was God's only
way of dealing with it.

Samuel's prophetic status was increasingly recognized (3:19-
21). Hebrew realism appears in the declaration that the Lord
would not let Samuel's words "fall to the ground." Because the
word of a man was a concrete thing, with his essential character
in it, one's dynamic intentions towards another could be made
effective in the other's life by words. This was the secret of the
prophetic belief that if a prophet spoke God's word, that dynamic
word was full of divine content, with the divine purpose of judgment and mercy in it. Its very utterance into a situation would set
to work those forces which would accomplish the divine plan.
Through his servant Samuel, the Lord's oracular presence was
recognized at Shiloh as "the LORD revealed himself to Samuel at
Shiloh by the word of the LORD." The true prophet was marked
uniquely by his possession of the divine word, a distinction to
cause much trouble later in the differentiation of true from false
prophets (see Jer. 14:14; 23:30-32).

The Fortunes of the Ark (4:1—7:1)

The Loss of the Ark (4:1-22)

Defeated by the Philistines at Aphek, a location not definitely
identified but probably in the Plain of Sharon near Hydda, the
Israelites staged a comeback by sending to Shiloh for the Ark.
The way the decision is phrased (4:3) indicates that, for them,
the presence of the Ark in their midst meant the presence of the
Lord himself, the God who had covenanted with them on Sinai's
height and whose personal being was extended in this visible symbol of his kingship over his people. When the Ark arrived, the
Israelite host uttered a loud cry of exultation. The cry may actually have been the customary war cry in all the wars of the Lord
—"Arise, O LORD, and let thy enemies be scattered; and let them
that hate thee flee before thee" (Num. 10:35). The tumultuous
cry seems to have struck fear into the Philistines, who remembered how the Israelites' God had fought for them before. The

Philistines declared that nothing like this had happened before, the reference apparently being to the presence of the Ark in battle. This enigmatic utterance is not supported by the evidence. Either by intention of the author or through corruption of the text, the Philistines are recorded as locating the plagues on the Egyptians as having taken place in the wilderness. The Philistines recovered their courage at the point of desperation and routed Israel decisively, capturing the Ark and slaying Eli's two sons.

The fact that a man of Benjamin carried the tragic news to Shiloh (4:12) would suggest that tribes other than Ephraim were involved in this battle; it was probably a united Israelite effort. The messenger's encounter with the blind Israelite leader, Eli, is dramatically told. The message realistically recounts the disasters that have befallen Israel, with their climax in the loss of the Ark. Eli and Phinehas' wife, who was in the throes of childbirth, were successive victims of the tragic news. The latter's son was named Ichabod, a name which indicated that the glory of the Lord, his visible presence among his people, had departed with the capture of the Ark.

The word "glory" is a characteristic term in Hebrew idiom for expressing the honor or splendor of a subject; it is that which evokes response and lends weight to a person or thing. The Ark was the special dwelling place of God's glory, his manifest presence in Israel, and as such it was also itself the glory of Israel, for God's presence in it gave Israel its pre-eminence. What finally caused Eli's collapse was the news, not that his sons were dead, but that the Ark was captured. God's glory had departed from his people and, with that departure, Israel's glory had gone too. Israel had nothing left to elevate it above its neighbors, for its glory was not in its man power or its riches but in the presence of its God. In the New Testament, Christ in us is said to be the "hope of glory," since it is the presence of his Spirit which gives significance to our lives and assures our future (Col. 1:27).

The Ark in the Hands of the Philistines (5:1-12)

The Ark was taken to Ashdod, one of five cities which constituted the Philistine federation, situated on the coastal plain about five miles from the Mediterranean Sea. Here the Ark was set up in the temple of the Philistine deity Dagon, beside the latter's image. The story presents the Lord as challenging a divine rival, and thus it reinforces the absolute claims of God evidenced in the

first commandment of the Decalogue and manifested throughout
the historical revelation. The living God will brook no rival. In
demonstration of this fact Dagon was twice left prostrate, and the
second time severely damaged.

Zephaniah 1:9 mentions a custom of leaping the threshold, and
this story gives the traditional origin of the custom. The broken
image of Dagon fell across the threshold of the temple and therefore the priests had to leap the threshold to enter.

The disaster to Dagon, who is identified with his image in the
story as he would have been by the Philistines, was followed by
sickness among the Ashdodites. In consequence the Ark was
taken to Gath. A similar pestilence led to yet a further removal
to Ekron. The pestilence was one of boils, but, as we shall see in
the next chapter, these appear to have been associated with mice,
which suggests that the disease was bubonic plague. The Philistines saw their trouble as the direct activity of the Lord, proving
his supremacy over Dagon, and anxiously sought for a way to
restore the Ark of the Lord to its place.

The Return of the Ark (6:1—7:1)

The Philistines consulted their priests and diviners, who advised
returning the Ark to Israel with an appropriate guilt offering. Once
more we see the priestly office associated with divination. The
priest was the guardian of the oracle among the peoples of the
Near East. It was usual in the case of a "guilt offering" (6:3) to
give reparation. Here it was to consist of five golden models of the
boils which had afflicted the Philistines, together with five golden
mice. The association of mice with boils is explained in the ancient
Greek translation of this section, which indicates that a plague of
mice swarmed across the land in connection with the plague of
boils. If the word "mice" is representative of the divers pestilential
rodents which carried the bubonic plague, the association is explained. The number of these golden images, five of each, was
based on the number of cities and princes which constituted the
Philistine confederation. There may have been an element of sympathetic magic in the gift of these images, the belief that if they
were sent out of the country, then the ills which they represented
would also disappear.

There remained the difficult issue of conveying the Ark back to
Israel. By taking two cows from their calves, the Philistines argued
that they could divine whether the Ark was really causing their

trouble. The Ark was to be drawn by the cows, who were yoked to it. The calves were to be left at their sides, and then at the last moment taken away and penned up. The cows would naturally turn in the direction of the calves when allowed to move, and if they did, then the association of the Ark with the trouble in Philistia was pure chance. But if the cows acted contrary to nature and conveyed the Ark back to Israel, then the holiness and power of the Lord would be disclosed, and it would be evident that it was he who had sent the pestilence. When the cows took the latter course, the Philistines were confident that their trouble was of divine origin and that they were right in making their golden images to "give glory to the God of Israel," that is, to acknowledge his power and supremacy (vs. 5).

The cows drew the Ark back to the land of Israel to Bethshemesh, and came to the field of a man named Joshua, who was reaping his wheat harvest. The men of Bethshemesh left their reaping and joyfully sacrificed the cattle which had drawn the visible seat of God's invisible presence back into their midst. We are told that the Levites offered the sacrifice, but this is probably a later addition to the text, coming from the days when the priests did not merely direct but alone administered sacrifices. The fact that the sacrifice was made upon a great stone is a reminder that an altar had to be improvised. Against it the blood of the slain beasts would be poured out to God and on it the carcasses would be burned.

The end of the chapter records a tragic concomitant. We are told that many men were slain because they looked on the Ark. The number of men (see margin) seems incredible and the reason for the judgment is difficult to understand since looking *on* the Ark (the correct rendering of the Hebrew) was not an offense. Here the Greek translation helps us. It tells us that seventy men were slain because they did not rejoice with the rest when they looked on the Ark. The number is more reasonable, even though the reason is still somewhat unintelligible. Probably the same pestilence struck which had struck the Philistines and which could have been carried in the Ark. The Hebrew author, convinced that all suffering was inextricably bound up with sin, sought for a theological answer. Such was certainly the hard-core doctrine of the Deuteronomists who were responsible for the writing of the Books of Samuel. The effect of this disaster was the removal of the Ark to Kiriath-jearim, a Canaanite city, possibly located nearby.

Samuel's Day of Power (7:2—8:22)

Samuel as Judge (7:2-17)

We are told that the Ark remained twenty years at Kiriath-jearim. The story now returns to Samuel, and the scene changes from Shiloh to Mizpah. In the original source there may have been some account of the destruction of Shiloh, but we are left with the mystery of its disappearance. In a speech which echoes the Deuteronomic framework of the Book of Judges, Samuel arraigns the Israelites on the ground that they have fallen away from the true worship of the Lord into the pagan ways of their Canaanite neighbors. They worship the fertility gods and goddesses, "the Baals and the Ashtaroth" of Canaan. Samuel calls for absolute and undivided loyalty to the Lord, and summons the people to Mizpah, about five miles north of Jerusalem. Jeremiah, in the last years of his ministry, had contact with Mizpah (Jer. 40:6), and he preserves the memory of Samuel as a man of prayer (Jer. 15:1), a memory authenticated in this story where Samuel offers to pray for Israel. We have to remember that the function of a prophet was twofold—to declare the will of God and to intercede with God for the people. Oracle and prayer both played a part in the prophet's ministry, thus showing that the prophet was much more akin to the priest than has often been allowed, a truth supported by the fact that the priest was also associated with oracular consultation, though with a different type. Samuel, trained to be a priest at Shiloh, here emerges also as a prophetic leader. Jeremiah with his emphasis on prayer stands in the same tradition (Jer. 29:7; 42:2, 20).

The penitence of the people was acted out symbolically by the pouring out of water. There was no law enjoining this, although we need to remember that water was a precious thing in the Near East, and there is a parallel in II Samuel 23:16 (see comment). The people of Israel fasted, showing penitence and acknowledging sin.

The gathering of the Israelites at Mizpah also brought together the Philistine hosts, always on watch for a possible resurgence of Israelite power. The craven Israelites were encouraged by Samuel, who is now described as judge (7:6). Once more a charismatic personality was to lead Israel. Samuel, the prophet-priest-judge, directed the burnt offering, possibly as the beginning of a military campaign (see Judges 6:20, 26; 20:26), and sought to allay the fears of his compatriots. The narrative seems somewhat telescoped. We may assume that battle was joined, but that a terrible storm swept the Philistines away in defeat. The Hebrew word for "voice" (7:10) is also a word for "thunder" and the latter was often interpreted in those early days as the direct intervention of the Lord himself. The "Stone of help," Ebenezer (7:12, see margin), set up by Samuel near the place of victory, was a victory marker.

In verses 13 and 14 we come on difficulty. There is every indication that the triumph over the Philistines was by no means so complete as these verses imply. The Philistines continued to invade the land of Israel, as the stories of Saul show. This short passage, out of keeping with the early tradition, is usually attributed to the Deuteronomic editors of First Samuel, who thus sought to glorify Samuel as the last great judge. Undoubtedly, however, the Israelites did win a notable victory near Mizpah.

Samuel's judgeship appears to have carried him on a regular annual circuit, centering in Ramah but passing through Bethel, Gilgal, and Mizpah. Thus the judgeship was now understood as a true rule, rather than simply as leadership in war and the championing of the oppressed. Samuel administered justice, and since the shrines were centers of such activity, we can understand both Samuel's right to do this, as prophet and priest, and his choice of the three centers, since each had a local sanctuary.

The Demand for a King (8:1-22)

At this point the demand for a king is first clearly heard. We have two conflicting traditions. The first, recorded in this chapter and in I Samuel 10:17-27a; 12:1-25, is critical of the monarchy, regarding it as contrary to the divine will for Israel and the result of the worldly desire of Israel to be like other peoples. The second, recorded in chapter 9, ascribes the kingship directly to the divine initiative and regards the monarchy as under the divine blessing. In one tradition, Samuel is represented as reluctantly granting a kingship to which he is opposed, and in the other, as actively giving the divine support to the project. The two cannot be reconciled, and it is generally believed that the first tradition, enshrined in the chapter now being considered, was a later one, reflecting many years of disappointing experience of the monarchy and embodying the teaching of prophets like Hosea, who regarded

the kingship as a manifestation of the divine wrath (Hosea 13:
11). Actually the two traditions are historically valuable. They
show us the presence of both pro- and anti-monarchical elements
in Israel. We may note that the opposition to the monarchy comes
out in the stories of Saul and not in the stories of David, and further that intense opposition to the monarchy, as with Hosea, appears to have emerged more in the Northern Kingdom where the
Davidic line of monarchy was not retained. It seems clear that
there was a genuine prophetic opposition to the monarchy, and
the so-called "late" tradition may preserve a genuine memory of
some misgiving in Samuel himself. Its picture of Samuel does not
represent him as entirely opposed to the monarchy, and, reading
between the lines, we sense a tension in the prophet's own thought.
Thus the story records the fact that Samuel was angry with God
when the Lord announced that he had cast off Saul, almost as if
Samuel really had hopes that the monarchy would succeed (I
Sam. 15:10-11). Furthermore, the prophet is presented as anointing David without any apparent opposition to the idea of kingship
(I Sam. 16:1-13). Evidently genuine tradition is preserved here,
however it may have been shaped by a later intense opposition to
the monarchy.

The maladministration of justice by Samuel's sons is cited as
the occasion for a popular demand for a king. Evidently Samuel
had handed on his governmental activity to his family. The tradition preserving this statement is prophetic and thus would be
strongly against injustice of rulers; yet it strangely ignores the un-
just sons of Samuel and condemns the people for making a way of
escape. We can understand this if the popular demand was later
seen as a rejection of God's direct kingship. As men became disillusioned with the monarchy, the thought of the king as God's
vicegerent, a very extension of the Lord's own personal being,
might have been accompanied by misgivings. Indeed, as we have
suggested, even in Samuel's mind misgiving may have been present. However, Samuel's speech, describing what a king would be
like, savors of long experience of the monarchy with its inevitable
adjuncts of forced labor, taxation, and military conscription. The
speech may well reflect the attitude of the Deuteronomic editors,
for Deuteronomy 17:14-20 offers a somewhat similar critical cata-
logue of regal rights. The statement of verses 11-18 offers a valuable summary of the place and rights of the kingship in Israel.

Despite the divine opposition expressed through the prophet, the popular demand persisted, and Samuel was told to seek a king. The people describe the task of the king more in terms of military leadership than in terms of civil administration and justice.

THE TRAGEDY OF SAUL

I Samuel 9:1—31:13

Saul as King (9:1—12:25)

The Choice of Saul and His Anointing (9:1—10:16)

Here we come to a second document about the kingship, setting it in a much more favorable light. Saul is represented as the son of Kish, a prosperous farmer. Saul was sent in search of some straying asses belonging to his father. The itinerary of the search is described in detail, although the place names are still a puzzle to archaeologists. Weary with the search, Saul and his servant, after traversing the land of Benjamin, turned to what would appear to be Ramah, since it is described as the dwelling place of Samuel, the man of God.

At this point we have an interesting insight into one of the prophetic roles. Saul regarded Samuel as a professional consultant who would divine for a fee. The prophetic nomenclature has retained three names in Hebrew to describe a prophet; two of these are translated "seer," and the emphasis in them falls on vision and audition. The third name, translated "prophet," originally seems to have described an ecstatic type of prophet who was thrown into abnormal psychical and physical states, performed extraordinary acts, and often spoke in an unintelligible tongue. In verse 9 we are told that this third word "prophet" had, at the time of writing, become the inclusive term, so that a "seer" was now a "prophet." Attempts have been made to differentiate absolutely between the two types. In such attempts the seer is said to be a solitary individual and the ecstatic prophet a gregarious one; the seer prophesies to order, whereas the ecstatic prophet has to be stimulated. Actually all such differentiations are unsafe. For example, Samuel is a seer when he is consulted by Saul, and yet he is also found in the company of ecstatics with their abnormal behavior and dances (19:18-24). It was out of this strangely varied background that the later canonical prophets like Amos, Hosea, Isaiah, and Jeremiah emerged. Often they received their messages as seers did, by sights presented to the eye or by sounds coming to the ear; but they also disclose the abnormal characteristics of the ecstatic type (Isa. 20:2; Ezek. 3:14-15; 4:4; chs. 8-11).

The city apparently had one gate, and its shrine or high place would be situated at its highest point, with a hall adjoining in which the cultic feasts would be eaten. Saul and his servant arrived when a special sacrificial feast was being celebrated. It is an interesting point that Samuel was to preside over this, an indication that priestly and prophetic roles were closely intertwined in these early days. The feast was associated with the type of sacrifice in which the blood of the sacrificial victim was poured out at the foot of the altar as a gift to God, the flesh being broiled and partaken of by the worshipers. In this way God and the worshipers communed together through the life of a third party, the sacrificial beast.

Samuel had been divinely warned beforehand that a Benjaminite whom God had appointed as king would arrive. Here we find an emphasis on Samuel's capacity for insight into the divine mind and purpose, a capacity which was God-given and which is central in the whole biblical revelation. When Saul arrived, he was identified in Samuel's prophetic consciousness as the divine appointee and was given the place of honor at the feast, over his own protest. So sure had Samuel been of the divine purpose as testified to in the deeps of his spirit, that he had delayed the feast until the promised visitor arrived.

Saul was put to sleep on the roof as was customary in the hot climate, and in the morning the prophet communicated to him the divine message. The giving of the oracle was followed by a private anointing as king, after even Saul's servant had been sent away. The term "anointed" was especially applied to Israel's monarch, and the practice of anointing with oil as an indication of the Lord's choice was the normal practice at the consecration of kings. Since the same practice was also employed for priests, this is a reminder that, like them, the king was a holy person, possessing charismatic qualities because he was divinely chosen and endowed. From now on, the king made a third with the priest and the prophet in the inner hierarchy of Israel's religious life.

As a sign of Saul's divine appointment, Samuel warned him that on his homeward journey, at the tomb of Rachel near Bethel, he would meet two men who would inform him that his father's asses had been found. He was then to change his route to go to the oak of Tabor. Here three men carrying varied provisions would supply him with bread, and he would pass on to "the hill of God," Gibeathelohim (Gibeah). Here there was a holy place where the Lord was worshiped, even though the place seems to have been in the Philistine sphere of influence and to have had a Philistine officer or prefect to collect tribute (according to the best meaning of the Hebrew word translated "garrison"). Saul would meet a band of prophets descending from this high place, and would himself experience the same possession by the Spirit which they were manifesting.

At this point we meet, for the first time specifically in the biblical text, the "dervish" type of prophet. These prophets, whom we have already described as ecstatics, banded themselves together and showed many abnormal characteristics. They appear to have been thrown into a frenzy and to have prophesied when the convulsive state was on them. They carried musical instruments, often as an aid to the stimulation of this abnormal state. We find their counterparts elsewhere in the ancient world, but the comparison is only superficial. Beneath their extraordinary forms of conduct and frenzied fanaticism, they often carried a real zeal for the Lord, were the exponents of pure religion, and were the bearers of authentic divine messages which they fearlessly declared. Not only Samuel but also Elijah and Elisha were associated with such bands, and they made a lasting and significant contribution to the prophetic tradition of Israel.

We are told that Saul experienced a change of heart on leaving Samuel. Already (in vs. 6) Samuel had promised that, when the Spirit took possession of him, he would be turned into another man, and this process is represented as beginning already. What Samuel had foretold now came to pass. Saul fell in with the band of prophets at Gibeah; the Spirit of God came mightily upon him; and he was thrown into a frenzy of ecstatic utterance, so much so that a proverb arose from the experience—"Is Saul also among the prophets?" The saying was an indication that a complete change had been wrought in Saul's personality.

This section does not finish with Saul's meeting Samuel, as Samuel had promised, but with the future king in conversation with his uncle, still keeping secret the matter of his kingship.

The Election at Mizpah (10:17-27)

Suddenly the scene changes from Gibeah to Mizpah, and we
return to the other and later tradition already partly recorded in
chapter 8. Samuel called the people together at Mizpah, address-
ing them in terms with which that chapter has already made us
familiar and treating the desire for a human king as a direct rejection of the direct kingship of God himself. Reluctantly he summoned them before God according to their tribes, that the divine
choice might be made known by the casting of the lot. The lot
fell on Benjamin, and when the clans of the tribe of Benjamin presented themselves, the lot fell on the clan of Matri. From this
clan, the family of Kish was chosen, and finally the lot fell on
Saul. He is represented as upstanding and warriorlike in appearance, so that the people hailed him with acclamation, after he
had been discovered hiding among the baggage and was brought
before them. That he hid among the baggage raises difficulties, as
does the mode of the oracular divination by which his hiding
place was discovered. He must have appeared in person for the
lot to fall on him, and surely immediate acclamation as king would
have followed. Some interpreters, in consequence, dismiss verses
21b and 22 from the text.

The method of sacred lot was used much in this period of Hebrew history. It was associated with the ephod and also the Urim
and Thummim. As noted in the Book of Judges, the ephod was
sometimes an image but it might also have been a special priestly
garment or an appurtenance associated with the sacred dice
(Judges 8:27; 17:5). These latter were apparently Urim and
Thummim. They may have been two stone tablets, one face of
each black and the other white. When cast, the decisions "yes"
and "no" would be associated with the turning up on each of the
same colored face, but if one came up white and the other black
no decision could be determined.

Saul was proclaimed king; Samuel outlined the duties and rights
of kingship to the assembled people; and the people were sent
home.

Saul's Opportunity: The Relief of Jabesh-Gilead (11:1-15)

Saul's opportunity for leadership came first of all against
Nahash and his Ammonites, who were laying siege to Jabesh-
gilead. This group of Semitic people appear also in the Book of

Judges, where they are seen to be Bedouins, living on the fringe of
the desert and continually raiding the more civilized area (Judges
3:13; 11:4). Nahash's object appears to have been to offer a contemptuous insult to Israel, probably prompted by overweening
confidence. The messenger sent out from Jabesh arrived at Gibeah
just as Saul returned from work in the fields. This is hardly consonant with what had happened at Mizpah, and the story fits in
much better with the earlier story of 10:1-16. Indeed, this was the
opportunity which Samuel had assured Saul would come to him.
Saul met the messenger by chance, and there is no hint that the
men of Gibeah knew that he had been chosen king or that they
looked to him for leadership. Nahash's confident challenge was
met by Saul, fresh from the experience at Gibeah and its trans-
forming influence. Once more the Spirit of the Lord came upon
him, and he was filled with a flaming fury, both against Nahash
and against any defaulting Israelites. He took symbolic action by
cutting up a yoke of oxen, sending the dismembered pieces
throughout Israel, and declaring that he would do likewise to the
oxen of any craven fellow countrymen. A strong host assembled,
and the Ammonites were utterly routed.

The result of Saul's triumph was a public confirmation of
Samuel's secret anointing. Verses 12-14 appear to be an editorial
effort to reconcile the two traditions. They refer to Saul's opponents, the "worthless fellows" of 10:25-27, and also to the ceremony at Mizpah which is now to be renewed. As we have seen, it
is difficult to reconcile the latter with the story just recounted. In
verse 15 we return to this story. Here Samuel does not appear, but
Saul is publicly made king at Gilgal with a sacrificial feast of
peace offerings and amid general rejoicing. Yet even here we have
an indication that the kingship was the desire of the people as well
as a divine appointment through the prophet, showing that the
two traditions give different facets of the one truth.

Samuel's Farewell Address (12:1-25)

This speech belongs to the second and later tradition, and is
paralleled by Joshua's farewell address in Joshua 24. The speech
continues the emphasis of 10:17-27. Samuel reminded his hearers
that he had gone along with them in the election of a king, and
now he offered his apologia. He made no mention of the misde-
meanor of his sons, but affirmed his honesty in the discharge of
his judgeship, listing the errors into which he might have fallen.

He had not defrauded or oppressed the Israelites, nor had he taken a bribe to let a murderer go free (the word for "bribe" here applies specifically to this kind of case).

Samuel followed up the declaration of innocence by a survey of Israel's past history. The Deuteronomic cycles of sin and judgment, repentance and mercy, already disclosed in the framework of Judges, are here delineated in summary form. The Lord's deliverance of his people can be described as his "saving deeds"; in them he manifests his righteousness by delivering the oppressed. The prophets saw the Lord as a righteous God *and* a Savior (Isa. 45:21). Now Israel's greatest sin has been committed. The antimonarchial theme appears, as Samuel arraigns the people for choosing a king to put in the place of the Lord. Yet all may still be well if they and their king obey God and walk in his ways. If they do not, then the hand of God will be against them in judgment.

As a sign that his message was authentic Samuel called for what was a miracle in Palestine—rain during the harvest. The latter rains preceded the harvest and then normally no more came until the autumn. The sign was given, a thunderstorm which was a manifestation of God's presence in judgment and in mercy. We have here yet another reminder of how, in these early days, the natural phenomena of lightning and thunder, storm and fire, could become extensions of the divine Presence, disclosing and also veiling God's glory.

The people's repentance, as this miraculous rain descended, met with a twofold response on Samuel's part. The first was the injunction that the true worship of the Lord must be preserved, even under the new conditions of a monarchy. The second was the affirmation that they were God's Chosen People, and that he would not cast them off, because he had chosen them and must abide true to himself and to his choice. This is the meaning of the phrase "for his great name's sake." God's name is himself, and God must be true to his own character. If God is righteous, he must abide by the norm that is himself; he cannot belie himself. If he has chosen Israel, then he will abide by his choice, even in his judgment on his people. At this point, Samuel stopped short, and it was left for the later prophets to hope for a divine righteousness which, *through* judgment, would work redemption for Israel, a hope fulfilled in Jesus and his Church, the New Israel.

We notice how the prophetic function of intercession is reaffirmed. Samuel offered his services as intercessor for the people. This was his duty under God. To forego praying for his fellows would be sin against God. Prayer was now the most effective aspect of his ministry, for by it the floodgates of heaven's mercy must be opened.

The Revolt Against the Philistines (13:1—15:35)

Preparations for War, and the Breach Between Saul and Samuel (13:1-23)

Despite his farewell speech, and perhaps because of its miraculous accompaniment, Samuel's influence in public affairs continued, as this chapter shows. Here we return to the early tradition of 9:1—10:16; 11:1-15. The Philistine menace now became serious. Philistine oppression was heavy and extended to economic monopolies. The editorial formula in verse 1 gives Saul's age and the duration of his reign; details have been omitted from the text so that the age and the duration are alike not clear. This formula characterizes the introduction to all later reigns in the Deuteronomic history of Samuel and Kings.

Saul's son Jonathan is now brought into the story, which shows a tendency to confuse Gibeah with Geba, situated only three miles away. The word translated "garrison" is better rendered "officer" or "prefect" (vss. 3-4; see also comment on 10:5). In 10:5 this officer is stationed at Gibeah, not Geba. Geba, it has been suggested, was the center for Jonathan. The latter's defeat of the Philistine officer at Gibeah precipitated a general uprising. Israel was summoned to Saul at Gilgal, while presumably Jonathan took command of the forces already in the field. The latter were soon opposed by a vastly superior Philistine host which gathered at Michmash, situated across from Geba and separated from it by a deep valley. The size of the Philistine army apparently caused an Israelite stampede.

At this point, we return to the Samuel-Saul story interrupted at 10:16. In this story Samuel had instructed Saul to go to Gilgal and wait for him there (10:8). Now, some months after this instruction, we find Saul at Gilgal, waiting for the seven days that Samuel had appointed until the prophet arrived. This story, which is inserted somewhat incongruously in the narrative at this point, is accepted by most interpreters as a later addition. It is highly

probable that authentic tradition is involved and that Samuel and
Saul may well have clashed at Gilgal, but the chronological setting
of the incident is apparently not as we have it here, and we shall
treat it as an independent story. Samuel failed to turn up on time.
Saul became impatient and offered the sacrifices himself. Then
Samuel arrived and condemned Saul for his action. We note that
the ministry of the prophet took precedence over that of the king,
in the thought of this story. Apparently it is preserved as an indication of why the house of Saul was not allowed to continue and
the house of David was raised up. Saul had displeased the Lord
by disobeying the prophetic injunction. The story reflects the later
pretensions of the Levitical priesthood and shows no appreciation
for the king as a holy person with a significant place in Israel's
worship, such as seems to have held for the Davidic kings. It is
difficult, therefore, to estimate how much of this tradition is historically authentic. At least there was a striking breach at Gilgal
between Samuel and Saul, and some sacrificial issue was involved.
From here on Samuel began to look elsewhere than to the house
of Saul for a king.

We now return to Geba and find both Saul and Jonathan, showing that the Gilgal story is out of its chronological order. The
Israelite stampede left Saul with only six hundred men. Furthermore, Israel was in a helpless state from the lack of a native smith.
The Israelites were apparently dependent upon the Philistines for
the state of their arms, but we may doubt whether they were in
such dire straits as the passage in verses 19-22 indicates. The Hebrew text is very disorganized here and it seems difficult, in the
light of the victory over the Ammonites, to believe that the Israelites were as short of arms as is suggested by this insertion.

Jonathan's Exploit and Its Consequences (14:1-52)

This chapter continues the story of chapter 13 which, as we
have seen, has been interrupted by various insertions. Jonathan
and his armor-bearer attacked a Philistine outpost. Their strategy
was to make the Philistines believe that the Israelites were coming
out of their hiding places in the caves. Thus they hoped to create
a panic in which the enemy would turn on one another. The sign
they set for themselves was to be the way they were challenged by
the Philistine sentries. The words of the sentries indicated that
they should advance, and their strategy succeeded, aided by an
earthquake. Some commentators suggest that traitor Israelites,

who had fled to the Philistines, were set upon in the confusion resulting from Jonathan's surprise attack and the earthquake. If so,
apostate Israelites as well as Philistines were punished. When the
Israelites at Geba (vs. 16, *not* "Gibeah") saw the resulting confusion in the enemy camp, they thought a sizable detachment of
their own number was responsible and found to their surprise that
only Jonathan and his armor-bearer were absent. As they gathered
for battle, even those who had fled to hiding took fresh courage
and rallied to the advancing host.

The presence of the Ark raises issues, for according to our text
the Ark of Shiloh remained at Kirath-jearim until the time when
David removed it to Jerusalem (I Sam. 7:1-2; II Sam. 6:1-5). The
word translated "ark" here is rendered in the Greek translation
"ephod." If this be the correct translation, Abijah the priest was
present in his oracular capacity, and Saul was consulting the
oracle prior to going into battle. He summoned Abijah to bring,
not the Ark, but the ephod, containing the sacred dice. The injunction to the priest to withdraw his hand is then explicable in
terms of the ceremony of the sacred lot. The obvious confusion
of the enemy caused Saul not even to wait upon the oracle; so he
bade the priest withdraw his hand from the sacred receptacle.

Victory followed; even the traitor Israelites in the Philistine
camp now returned to their countrymen, and the Philistines were
routed to Beth-aven and beyond. Meanwhile Saul had laid a sacred
ban on his army. The soldiers were not to partake of food until
evening when the enemy had been routed. This fact had a religious basis. God was evidently fighting for his people, and they
must play their part to ensure his continued support. Jonathan,
absent on his mission and ignorant of Saul's ban, ate honey in the
forest, whereas his fellow Israelites passed by without putting the
hand to the mouth, fearing the dread consequences of the oath
they had sworn. Told of his father's ban, Jonathan obviously regarded this as a hindrance to complete victory. When evening
came, the hungry Israelites fell upon the beasts which they had
taken as spoil from the enemy, slaughtered them, and ate them
with their blood. We have to remember that, in Hebrew thought,
the blood was regarded as the bearer of the life-principle and thus
as especially sacred. It must not be consumed or just poured on
the ground, for it belonged to God, the giver of all life. In all
sacrifices the blood was drained from the beast and poured out as
a divine libation at the foot of the altar. In any slaughter the blood

must be disposed of in like manner. Indeed, most slaughters partook of the nature of sacrifice. Hence we have Saul's rebuke of
the people and his securing a stone, to take the place of an altar,
against which the blood might be poured.

Before further pursuit of the fleeing Philistines, Saul was encouraged by the priest to consult the divine oracle once more.
This time the sacred dice gave no answer, and Saul deduced that
there was sin in the camp. He required the oracular dice, now
described as "Urim" and "Thummim," to decide between the people on one side, and him and his son on the other. Exactly how
this casting of the dice was managed and what they were like remain shrouded in mystery. Urim and Thummim seem to mean
unanimity of positive and negative answers respectively. Saul and
Jonathan were taken, and further consultation placed the guilt on
Jonathan, who confessed to tasting the honey and who was prepared to die, despite the ignorance underlying his action. The people came to his support and pleaded for his life, with the result
that Jonathan was released and the pursuit of the fleeing
Philistines apparently ceased.

The chapter closes with a summary of Saul's victories over
various enemies of Israel, and a record of his family and of his
commands (vss. 47-52). We are reminded of his lifelong struggle
with the Philistines and of his ability to gather around him strong
and courageous warriors. This summary seems intended to close
Saul's reign, but the reign continues in subsequent chapters, and
we may conclude that it is a relic of the editing and re-editing
which the traditions must have undergone as the Books of Samuel
were being compiled.

The Rejection of Saul (15:1-35)

This chapter represents the later tradition, with its opposition
to the monarchy as contrary to the divine will, although there are
also reflections of a more favorable attitude, akin to that of the
early source, in verse 1 and subsequently in the chapter. These
references probably show that opposition to the monarchy does
go back to Saul's time, but that it was not so violent and one-sided
as the tradition was later shaped to indicate.

Saul was given divine instructions to destroy the Amalekites
because of their treatment of Israel in the wilderness journey. Apparently Samuel was still very much in evidence, and it is difficult
to place this chapter chronologically; the association with Samuel

suggests a point near Saul's anointing. The story may well embody the cause of the real break between the king and the prophet, namely, the way in which the campaign against Amalek was conducted.

The Amalekites were foes of Israel from the wilderness days. They led a seminomadic existence on the desert fringe of southern Palestine, occasionally raiding the cultivated areas in search of provisions, especially at harvest time. Judah was open to such raids because of its proximity to the Amalekite territory, and Saul singled out the men of Judah in the army which he gathered. The divine instructions to Saul through the prophet were that "Amalek," both the people and their property, was to be totally wiped out. This total extermination is known as a "ban," that is, a curse in which a whole people is to be destroyed because of the sin of some group within it. The verb "utterly destroy" is best translated "devote to destruction." The practice was bound up with the belief that Israel was the Chosen People of the Lord, a holy people, dedicated to their God. Other peoples had their own gods and were dedicated to them, therefore they would fall under the ban of the Lord. They could have no part in his holy purpose. They and their property must be destroyed before him. This "ban" evidently played a part in the invasion of Canaan and persisted down into the time of the monarchy. If a people could not share in the holiness of the Lord, they came under his ban. In the case of the Conquest and here also, the ban was not rigorously enforced. Intermarriage with the Canaanites rather than extermination was the dominant policy. In the same way, Saul apparently did not totally destroy the Amalekites, for enough were left to give trouble later (30:1). It may well be that the ban was carried out only in token form.

The Kenites were spared because of their kinship with Judah, a composite tribe which included Kenite elements, and because of the intermarriage of Moses with their group. Having warned this friendly tribe to depart, Saul turned on the Amalekites, wiping them out but sparing their king and their choicest cattle.

The Lord now declared that Saul had forfeited his kingship. Samuel, quite out of keeping with his general attitude as represented in this late tradition, was at first angry with God for this change of plan, but a night of prayer cleared his understanding. He went to Saul and reproved him for breaking the ban. Saul made the excuse that the choicest beasts were being kept for sacrifice to the Lord, but Samuel apparently rejected this plea and conveyed to Saul the divine message of rejection. Over the protests of Saul, the prophet reminded the king in a short oracle, paralleled in the pre-exilic prophets, that obedience to God's demands is more important in the divine eyes than sacrifice (vss. 22-23; see Hosea 6:6; Amos 5:21-24; Micah 6:6-8). Because Saul had disobeyed the Lord, he was rejected as king.

In view of the large part played by the practice of divination in these stories and Samuel's participation in it, the attack on the sin of divination either reflects the later prophetic condemnation of this sacred rite or is a mistaken rendering of the original text.

Saul's attempt at repentance met with no encouragement, and he and the prophet parted in a final break, after Samuel had slain Agag with his own hands. Verse 29 seems to contradict verses 11 and 35. It may well be, as some commentators suggest, that verses 24-31 were a later insertion.

Saul and David (16:1—20:42)

The Choice of Saul's Successor (16:1-13)

The present form of this story is probably late; it provides the inevitable sequel to the tradition preserved in the preceding chapter. The breach between Samuel and Saul led naturally to the choice of a candidate to replace Saul. The prophetic consciousness of Samuel was made aware of the divine will. God had rejected Saul as king and would provide his successor from among the sons of Jesse, the Bethlehemite. We may infer that divine inspiration directed Samuel's mind to the remembrance of this man, a devout worshiper of the Lord. Samuel went accordingly to Bethlehem and, as divinely directed, arranged for a sacrifice, to which Jesse and his family were invited. They were consecrated, presumably by ritual lustration, and as the sons passed before him, Samuel sought for a guiding sign. The sign was not given with seven of the sons, but the youngest, left behind to tend the flock, proved to be the divine choice, after he was summoned. He was duly anointed with oil by the prophet, and the Spirit of the Lord came upon him as previously it had done upon Saul. Once more the king is shown to be a charismatic personality, and thus kingship for Israel is demonstrated to be a religious as well as a political office. The gift of the Spirit is closely associated with the practice of anointing.

David Meets Saul (16:14-23)

Here we return to the early tradition. It describes how Saul became subject to an obscure mental affliction, producing extreme depression and attributed to an evil spirit, the Lord having withdrawn his Spirit and sent this in its place. We note again the Hebrew tendency to ignore secondary causes and ascribe everything, even evil things like madness, to direct divine activity. The belief that madness was due to demonic influence is present in the New Testament, as the ministry of our Lord shows, and the facts of demon possession and its curative exorcism were accepted by the Early Church. Just as ecstatic prophecy was often stimulated by musical accompaniments, so the effects of the evil power were amended by music. By this means David was brought to Saul's notice, as a practiced player on the lyre, able to soothe the king's depression. This story fits in with the tradition which regarded David as a musician and made him the typical figure around whom the psalmody of Israel was gathered across the succeeding centuries. David was engaged by Saul as his armor-bearer or squire.

David and Goliath (17:1—18:5)

In the preceding story David was described to Saul as a man of valor, a standing hardly consonant with his employment as armor-bearer and suggesting typical Eastern hyperbole among friends at court. We now come to an incident which is actually recorded in a highly complex story in which two traditions seem to have been combined. The story we have just looked at associates David with Saul as armor-bearer or musician. This early tradition is continued in chapter 17, but it is intermixed with a later tradition which began in 16:1-13 and which identifies David as a comely shepherd lad, not associated with Saul, and anointed by Samuel at Bethlehem. The early tradition is continued in 17: 1-11, 32-40, 42-48a, 49, 51-54, and the later tradition is preserved especially in 17:12-31; 17:55—18:5; and other single verses. In the second version, David was a shepherd boy, untrained in the arts of war, who was sent by Jesse with provisions for the older sons in Saul's army. He naïvely offered to meet singlehanded the giant who was terrorizing his countrymen. The story obviously knows nothing of David as Saul's armor-bearer, but emphasizes his status as a mere shepherd lad. Even his brethren have apparently not fully accepted his position as the Lord's anointed. At this point the second version finishes abruptly and is fitted into the first and earlier tradition contained in the first eleven verses of the chapter. No one reading the chapter carefully can avoid seeing the obvious combination here. At verse 32 David is once more Saul's armor-bearer and a man of valor. The armor was left behind as too cumbersome, and David took the field with the sling and stone so familiar in his former life as a shepherd boy. His strategy succeeded; the Philistine giant was stunned by the stone from David's sling and then killed by David with a sword. Verse 50 belongs to the later tradition and regards the giant as killed by David's stone. In this verse the picture of the shepherd boy returns, as also in verse 55 where David is obviously unknown to Saul and is not his armor-bearer. In this tradition the Goliath incident serves as a means of introducing David to Saul, and the version finishes with the developing friendship between David and Saul's son, Jonathan. David is taken into Saul's service and fitted out with Jonathan's armor, a common way of sealing a friendship.

We note the covenant friendship between David and Jonathan. This was a form of relationship made in the presence of the Lord, in which each party accepted obligations toward the other; it was regarded as being of the same order as blood relationship. It was such that it could be described as the knitting together of the souls of the two men (18:1), by which was meant that the very being of the one was extended into and embraced the personality of the other; each became the other's alter ego.

It is difficult to assess which of these two versions is closer to historical actuality. The Goliath incident was a turning point in the Philistine war; Jonathan's covenant with David is bedded deep in Israel's history; David's resourcefulness and his shepherd background seem beyond dispute; and his outwitting of Goliath is credible. David's actual mode of introduction to Saul is an issue, however, that remains in obscurity, although the early tradition of a relationship based upon David's ability as a musician fits in well with David's place in Israel's religious life as a typical master of psalmody.

David's Marriage and Saul's Mounting Jealousy (18:6-30)

The Greek version (Septuagint) omits 18:10-11, 17-19, 27-30, and probably is nearer the original. The omitted verses leave as a more consistent story the record of Saul's growing jealousy of David. On his return from battle, the women hailed David in terms that placed him above Saul and aroused the latter's jealousy. At first, Saul was afraid of David (vs. 12); then he stood in awe of him and tried to get rid of him (vss. 20-25); finally he was so afraid that he gave instructions for David's murder (19: 1). We have a picture of a tragic figure, brilliant in part but so egotistical that he can brook no possible rival. Among the means that Saul used to lure David to destruction was the offer of the hand of his daughter Michal in marriage. (If we follow the Greek translation, the incident relating to the elder daughter, Merab, was an alien intrusion into the story.) David's rejection of the offer on the ground of poverty was cunningly countered by Saul's request for a hundred Philistine foreskins. David responded more than successfully, bringing two hundred foreskins. His prestige as warrior mounted in Israel and was further enhanced by his marriage into the king's family. Here we have a fascinating psychological study. Saul had given David a task which was technically a promotion but which could also mean his destruction. Saul was thwarted and sought yet other means to rid himself of his hated rival. This is an authentic picture of the mounting jealousy of a deranged but brilliant mind.

Saul's Strategy and David's Escape (19:1-17)

It is generally assumed that this section belongs to the early armor-bearer-musician tradition concerning David. Saul now sought David's murder, but Jonathan's intercession led to a temporary truce between the king and his rival. The covenant bond between the two young men stood firm, and Jonathan's affection for his friend provided a protection against Saul's jealousy.

War against the Philistines broke out again, and presumably David's further success here aroused a fresh outburst of envy in Saul. The story of Saul's throwing a spear, already recorded in 18:10-11 but omitted by the Septuagint, is probably here in its proper place. David fled from the mad king, aided by Michal who placed a "teraphim" (19:13, margin), a household image, in the bed in his place. The Eastern habit of covering the head when asleep would delay identification (vs. 13).

The identification of the obscure word "teraphim" as an image in this passage raises a question. This image presumably was life-size, but when Rachel stole her father's "teraphim," again obviously images, they were sufficiently small to be hidden in a camel's saddle (Gen. 31:31-35). This story of David is evidence of the persistence of household gods or idols, even in the royal house that was dedicated to the worship of the Lord, a reminder both of the long struggle for a pure worship of the God of Israel against a pagan and polytheistic environment and of the need for the first command of the Decalogue.

The Events at Ramah (19:18-24)

This probably belongs to the late tradition of David as the shepherd boy secretly anointed by Samuel. It gives its own reason for the popular proverb, "Is Saul also among the prophets?", a reason quite distinct from that offered by the early tradition in 10:10-12.

David fled to Samuel at Ramah. Three times Saul sent messengers to apprehend David. Each time they were overtaken by the Spirit of God pervading the band of prophets around Samuel and David at Naioth, which was probably the name of the dwelling of the prophetic community at Ramah. Finally, Saul himself went, only to have the same experience befall him. Hence the proverb arose.

David and Jonathan (20:1-42)

This is an early narrative, although there are editorial additions, such as the first part of verse 1, obviously added to form a connecting link with the preceding story. The exact context of the events recorded is difficult to locate. They may well have occurred prior to David's marriage to Michal.

Jonathan, covenanted to his friend, was persuaded to discover the specific reason for his father's enmity to David. The story is developed with Jonathan's protestation that his father kept no secrets from him and that David had exaggerated Saul's hatred for him. David stressed Saul's knowledge of Jonathan's affection for his friend and hence his tendency to keep from Jonathan any indication of his true attitude toward David. He pleaded that his own life was at stake, and Jonathan, persuaded of the serious situation in which his friend was placed, agreed to discover his father's mind.

David's strategy was bound up with the annual festival of the new moon, when David's family were to sacrifice and feast together at Bethlehem. This was to be David's excuse for a breach of etiquette, that is, nonattendance at the royal table. Saul's reaction to David's absence would show his true attitude. If he condoned the absence, all was as Jonathan had said. If he were angry, then Jonathan must discover the cause.

We note David's emphasis on the covenant bond, with his plea that Jonathan keep faith (20:8). The mark of a covenant was the quality of constancy and loyalty between the parties involved and the requirement that there be a steadfast love between them.

Jonathan indicated to David the sign by which he was to know the verdict. David was to hide in a field. Jonathan would shoot three arrows. If they fell short of the mark, David's suspicions were ungrounded, but if they fell beyond the mark, David was to flee for his life. Jonathan regarded his discovery of his father's attitude as within the will of God, and could describe the possibility of David's flight from Saul's anger as within the divine intention—the Lord would have sent him away (20:22). Here we have a manifestation of typical Hebrew faith like that which led Joseph to affirm that even though his brethren had planned evil against him, God had intended it for good and overruled his misfortune (Gen. 50:20). A deep insight that applies to us all!

At the same time Jonathan required of his friend a like steadfastness of faith with himself and his house in loyal love forever, in harmony with their covenant (20:14-15). Once more the interlocking of personalities within the covenant bond is stressed in the declaration that Jonathan loved David as he loved his own soul, that is, as himself (20:17).

When Saul, Jonathan, and Abner sat down at table, the king noted the absence of the fourth regular member of the party. When the reason for David's absence was given, Saul's rage knew no bounds, and he even turned upon Jonathan. The issue of Jonathan's succession to the kingdom was evidently central in the king's mind (vs. 31). Jonathan hastened out to warn David by the agreed sign, and, when his servant had returned to the city, bade his covenant-friend affectionate farewell.

Civil War (21:1—26:25)

David's Visit to Nob (21:1-9)

This story probably follows close on the Michal episode and David's escape from Saul's messengers (19:12). David arrived at

Nob where he was received by Ahimelech the priest. Apparently Nob had become an important cultic center, the glory of Shiloh having faded with the departure of the Ark. Ahimelech's suspicions were quieted, even though David was alone, by the latter's false explanation. David declared that his mission was so secret that even his followers had to gather at a rendezvous. The subterfuge worked so well that David secured for himself alone enough bread to feed his fictitious companions. In addition, he explained the absence of weapons as due to his haste, and received the sword of Goliath. The ethics of this maneuver cannot be defended, but we find the resort to falsehood quite often in the early source to which this story belongs—a reminder of the lower stage of morals at this period of Israel's history. Here David's action goes uncondemned.

The bread Ahimelech offered David was holy, not profane; that is, it was separated for use at the sanctuary in the service of God. It was "the bread of the Presence." As such it partook of the quality of the Lord with whose worship it was associated, and could not be touched or eaten except with appropriate ritual purification. To eat the holy bread was equivalent to taking part in a sacrificial meal and communing with the Deity. Hence Ahimelech inquired whether David and his fictitious followers had "kept themselves from women," for sexual intercourse brought ceremonial uncleanness. David's plea that such acts were banned by the very nature of their warlike enterprise is a reminder that, in the early days, war was most often a divine venture, undertaken only after a sacrifice had been made to the Lord, and requiring ritual consecration on the part of the warriors (see Deut. 23:9-11).

Unfortunately for Ahimelech and his priests, the chief of Saul's herdsmen, Doeg the Edomite, was a witness to the transaction. He is described as "detained before the Lord," an indication that he was ceremonially unclean and was undergoing a period of purification prior to taking part in some religious ceremony. His presence was to have a tragic sequel.

David Flees to Achish (21:10-15)

This story belongs to the later tradition, and thus is not connected with the preceding section, which is continued in chapter 22. The early tradition to which that section belongs reports David's visit to Gath in chapter 27:1-12 as if it were his first. The connection of the present section with the preceding one is also made difficult by the fact that chapter 21 leaves David with the sword of Goliath in his possession, hardly a weapon with which to flee into the Philistine area. The story now under review is probably a parallel to the story of 27:1-12, but one which sets David in a more favorable light as no ally of the Philistines. If this be correct, the story is here out of place and belongs later, with chapter 27.

David fled to Gath, was recognized by Achish, the king of the Gathites, and was taken into custody. He adopted the ruse of feigning madness, a state regarded as produced by spirit possession and hence to be treated with reverential caution. The ruse succeeded and David fled.

The Flight to Adullam (22:1-5)

We return now to the early tradition. David, in his flight from Saul, arrived at the cave ("stronghold" is a better translation) of Adullam, where he was joined by his brethren, his father's house, and many more who were fugitives for various reasons. In all, he gathered a bodyguard of about four hundred men. Adullam has been identified as a site about twelve miles southwest of Bethlehem, and thus was in Judah. David's father and mother were left in the keeping of the king of Moab, on whom David had a claim through his great-grandmother, the ex-Moabitess Ruth. The meaning of verse 5 is obscure.

The Priests of Nob (22:6-23)

Saul sat at Gibeah under the tamarisk tree at the high place, that is, under the sacred tree at the shrine, surrounded by his bodyguard composed of Benjaminites. He grumbled about the disloyalty of his servants and especially attacked Jonathan for the covenant with David. Doeg the Edomite, apparently having completed his ceremonial requirements at Nob, was standing by and seized the opportunity to report the action of Ahimelech. According to him, Ahimelech not only provided David with food and the sword of Goliath, but also consulted the oracle for him—a fact not reported previously in the story. The enraged king summoned Ahimelech and his priests to his presence. Ahimelech picked out the untrue part of Doeg's accusation and denied consulting the oracle. He professed ignorance of the breach between Saul and David. Saul condemned him, his priests, and his household to death, but the servants refused to carry out the command. Doeg then was ordered to undertake the task. Doeg slew Ahimelech, his retinue of priests, and their families, and destroyed Nob. One son of Ahimelech, Abiathar, escaped and fled to David. The priests are described as wearing the ephod, which means presumably that they were qualified to carry the sacred oracle, or ephod, of Nob. Abiathar evidently took this ephod with him, since he is described later as carrying it to David in his flight (23:6). This tragedy at Nob may be linked with the prophecy to Eli that disaster would overtake his family (2:31-36).

The Deliverance of Keilah (23:1-13)

The Philistine raids continued. David's military prestige was such that men turned confidently to him for help, even though he was an outlaw. One occasion was a Philistine raid on the threshing floors at Keilah. Having twice consulted the oracle, presumably Abiathar's ephod, and having received each time an affirmative answer, David followed the divine instructions and delivered Keilah by routing the Philistine invaders.

With David in Keilah and away from the stronghold of Adullam, Saul saw his opportunity for open battle. Once more David consulted Abiathar's oracle, asking in succession two questions. Since the oracle could only deal with one question at a time, we must presume that the first part of verse 11 is comprehensive and that the detailed asking is described in the latter part of verse 11 and in verse 12. The oracle indicated that Saul would descend on Keilah and that the men of Keilah would surrender David to Saul. Acting on the divine response to his consultation, David and his band departed from Keilah.

The Attempted Betrayal by the Ziphites (23:14-29)

The Ziphites, according to our records, twice attempted to betray David. It is probable that the story here and the one in chapter 26 are two versions of the same event. The version here is more formal and probably the later of the two.

David fled to the hill country, pursued by Saul, and sought refuge in the Wilderness of Ziph, to the south of Hebron. The Ziphites reported his presence in their area, but meantime David had been reassured by Jonathan, who continued loyal to his covenant. The Ziphites went on ahead of Saul to spy out David's hiding places, but David managed to elude Saul, being finally delivered when Saul received news of a new Philistine invasion and had to leave for home. David took refuge in the strongholds of Engedi.

David's Magnanimity at Engedi (24:1-22)

Returning from the Philistine digression, Saul pursued David into the fastness of Engedi. The reference to a cave amid the sheepfolds probably indicates a gathering of stone-walled enclosures for protecting the sheep from harsh weather near some cave in which the shepherds could take refuge. David and his men were hiding in the depths of the cave when Saul went in. As the king was squatting, with his cloak loose, David's men besought him to take Saul's life, but David, remembering that the king was a holy person, anointed by the Lord, contented himself with cutting off the skirt of Saul's cloak and refused to allow his men to attack the king. David saw a deeper import in the words of the Lord, quoted by his men, that his enemy would be delivered into his hand and he should do with him as he willed. This meaning was brought out in the conversation with Saul that followed. As Saul was leaving the cave, David disclosed himself, and urged Saul to recognize that he had no enmity or hatred in his heart, since he had spared the king when the latter's life was in his hand. As a proof, he showed the tailpiece of Saul's cloak, and once more he affirmed that he could not harm the person of the king, calling on God to judge between them as to whether he, David, harbored in his heart the enmity that Saul attributed to him. David quoted a proverb which indicated that if he were as Saul said, then he would have taken the king's life, for a wicked heart can produce only wicked deeds.

Here we see one of the fine ethical characteristics which marked the Hebrew faith and which found full expression in the teaching and life of our Lord himself (Matt. 5:38-48; Luke 6:27-31; Matt. 18:21-22; Luke 23:34). David's magnanimity finds its resting place in the justice of the Lord. God himself would judge David's cause, and David had no need to take punishment into his own hands.

Saul was apparently smitten by David's attitude and admitted that David was more righteous than he. The point here is not that David is more morally good, for "righteousness" in its root Hebrew sense means conformance to the norm of justice, and is thus a legal term. David had appealed to the righteous God to judge his cause and thus had referred the dispute to the bar of divine justice. Saul had taken the matter into his own hands and was therefore less righteous, deciding the issue without reference to the divine justice. Once more Saul, like Jonathan, made a plea that, when David became king, he would keep faith with Saul's descendants and not annihilate his family as was the customary practice.

David and Abigail (25:1-44)

The first verse is probably editorial, reporting the death of Samuel. David remained an exile in the south in the neighborhood of Ziph and Maon. The Carmel here mentioned is not the place later associated with Elijah (I Kings 18:20-40), but a place now located as "Kermel" in this southern area. Nabal, a rich man noted for his meanness, was holding his sheepshearing festival (compare Gen. 38:12). He is described as a Calebite, a member of a clan incorporated in the complex tribe of Judah. David's band had apparently been of service in protecting from marauders Nabal's flock, with its valuable wool, and now David sent his young men to ask for provisions in return for this protection. Apparently Nabal's own young men supported David's claim. Nabal, however, refused, and refused in a churlish way. David, angered at this attitude, set out with part of his band to annihilate the Calebite and his household.

Meanwhile one of Nabal's young men had reported the affair to Abigail, Nabal's wife, as beautiful and sensible as Nabal was churlish and mean. This servant gave credit to David for his unofficial protection of her husband's flocks and warned Abigail against the impending disaster. She at once gathered a quantity of provisions and sent them on ahead by the servant, she herself following to meet David. In pleading with the Israelite hero, she made play on Nabal's name which means "fool" and showed herself a mistress of words, contending that the annihilation of Nabal and his household would be a rash act that would recoil on David's own head. She maintained that David was fighting in the cause of the Lord, and would therefore be protected and his life preserved; his life would be "bound in the bundle of the living" under God's care. This is no reference to immortality but to God's providential care in this mortal life. Because David was God's servant, he must not soil his soul by taking justice into his own hands and carrying it on his conscience. He was appointed prince over Israel by the Lord and must leave justice to him. This David had already done in the case of Saul at Engedi.

David recognized the justice of Abigail's plea, once more revealing his superiority to the normal standard of conduct of his contemporaries. Abigail had been sent by God, and David had been restrained from bloodguilt. Abigail returned home, and, on her report to Nabal of what had transpired, the latter had what appears to have been a stroke following his bout of drunkenness. Nabal's death was interpreted by David as an indication of the rightness of his conduct in leaving his cause in the hands of the Lord. He claimed Abigail as his wife, remembering the plea she had herself made and also undoubtedly because of the personal impression she had made on him. Saul had already given Michal, David's first wife, to another.

David Spares Saul's Life (26:1-25)

Here we have the other form of the story of the Ziphites and probably the earlier, since it has a wealth of detail and freshness about it. The places mentioned are in the same general area as those in the story of chapter 24; the Ziphites play the same role; David spares Saul's life, although the details of the account are different.

David took one of his company, Abishai, and entered by stealth at night into the heart of Saul's encampment. They came upon Saul asleep in the heart of the camp. Abishai, in words similar to those used by David's followers in the earlier story, besought David to slay Saul. David, in like words, refused to take the life of the Lord's anointed one, and satisfied himself by taking Saul's spear and water jar. Once free of the camp and on the mountaintop, David shouted through the darkness, a detail which explains why, in the other version as in this, Saul recognized David by his voice and not by his appearance (24:16). He arraigned Abner, Saul's commander, for his faulty watch over his king, and offered the spear and water jar as testimony that Saul's life had been in his hands.

Saul, recognizing David's voice, was then addressed in the same form as in the other version of the incident, but there is one additional element here worthy of notice. This is the suggestion that to be banished from Israel's land means to serve other gods (vs. 19). Behind this lies the primitive notion that the

Lord was God over Israel's land only, and that in other nations their gods were supreme. Hence banishment meant to pass into the realm of some other deity. As the lofty monotheism implicit in the wilderness faith of Moses reached its full expression in the great canonical prophets, this popular idea was superseded. Some echo of it remained in the conviction that, just as Israel was God's Chosen People, so its land was his special delight; it was Beulah land, and here God chose to manifest his presence. This faith in the tabernacling presence of God was brought to a focus in the Temple at Jerusalem. Love of God's house, still a mark of Christian piety, is one expression of the truth implicit in this attitude. We need, moreover, to remember that God is known to be present *everywhere* because he has chosen to be especially present *somewhere*. That is the truth which was emphasized in the idea of the tabernacling presence in the "Holy of Holies" and which finally became actualized in the Incarnation.

The incident apparently ended, as in chapter 24, with some measure of reconciliation. Each went his way in peace.

The War with the Philistines (27:1—31:13)

David at Gath (27:1—28:2)

David now openly joined himself with the Philistines. We have suggested that 21:10-15 was probably a later version of the story to which we now turn our attention.

Achish of Gath, aware of the trouble between Saul and David, welcomed the latter as an ally and allowed him and his band to dwell at Ziklag. An outlaw from his own land, David was yet loyal to his own people and was careful not to raid Judah. He seems to have played a double game by raiding the Geshurites, the Girzites, and the Amalekites. The first two groups are difficult to identify, but the Amalekites were inveterate enemies of Judah. By this means, David actually placated the Judahites. At the same time, he pretended to the Philistines that he was attacking various groups of the tribe of Judah such as the Jerahmeelites or the Kenites or other inhabitants of the Negeb, the steppeland bordering the desert in the south of Judah. Thereby he pleased Achish. To carry the last subterfuge through, David exterminated totally the groups he attacked, so that none should survive to tell the story. So successful was David that Achish really believed that the Israelite hero was now abhorred by his own people. In consequence, the king of Gath sought to make him his bodyguard for life, and David appears guardedly to have accepted. He was soon to be tested, for the Philistines decided on a major attack on Israel.

The Witch of Endor (28:3-25)

The Philistines gathered at Shunem, and Saul gathered his opposing army at Gilboa. Now fears began to overtake the Israelite king. Since his priesthood had been eliminated at Nob and Samuel was dead, he had no legitimate means of consulting the divine will. So desperate was he that any device of foreseeing the future was better than none. There remained the ways of necromancy, but Saul had earlier driven all wizards and mediums out of the land. One medium, a witch at Endor, had survived; Saul decided to consult her, and to do so in disguise. Afraid of practicing her art because of what had happened to the others, the woman consented only on the assurance of the disguised king that no harm would befall her. Told to bring up Samuel, the woman recognized Saul (probably "Samuel" should be read "Saul" in verse 12), but when reassured she went on with the séance. The primitive Hebrew viewed the afterlife as a shadowy existence in "Sheol," the subterranean cavern where the dead slept their long sleep, irrespective of the social and moral distinctions of this life. This realm of shades included a weak and meaningless existence. In the popular mind, it was conceived as a place of shades and darkness where life became emptied out. Samuel's shade was to be brought up from this subterranean realm. The medium accomplished her task and ostensibly put Saul in contact with the dead prophet. Samuel's message was, if anything, more devastating than any utterance of his lifetime. God had forsaken Saul and taken from him his kingdom; disaster awaited him and his army at the hands of the Philistines; and David would receive the kingdom. We note that only the medium saw Samuel; Saul's reactions came after her description. The general form and setting tally with modern spiritualistic practice. Probably Samuel's voice was simulated by ventriloquism, and the speech represented as his gave the witch an opportunity to avenge herself on Saul for his treatment of her and her fellow magicians.

Saul, overcome by the devastating message, fell to the ground. It was with great difficulty that he was persuaded to take food, and he returned to his camp a stricken man. There is a moral

to the story. Spiritualism is often the last and damning resort of
those who have rejected the legitimate means of approaching God
and the divinely ordained channels of revelation.

David Escapes from a Dilemma (29:1-11)

The Philistine army gathered at Aphek, and in the military review
the Philistine "commanders" noticed the presence of David and
his Hebrews. Precedent had not been favorable to Hebrew mercenaries, for there was still fresh memory of those who had
deserted to Saul at Geba (14:21). Moreover, the Philistine leaders
knew of David's reputation as a warrior superior to Saul and as
a doughty opponent to their own forces. Achish might testify
to David's loyalty to himself and to his enmity to Saul, but this
did not allay the suspicion of the princes. Meantime the dilemma
must have become acute for David—how was he to avoid fighting against his own people and against the Lord's anointed one?
Fortunately the situation was now taken out of his hands. Under
pressure from the commanders, Achish withdrew David from
the battle array and sent him back to the land of the Philistines.
Although David dissembled by regarding the decision as a reflection upon his own loyalty to Achish, we can sense the relief
he must have felt. The location of Aphek appears to have been,
like Jezreel, in the Plain of Esdraelon.

The Annihilation of the Amalekites (30:1-31)

David returned to Ziklag only to discover that in the absence
of his armed band the Amalekites had seized the opportunity
to burn the city, carry away the women and children, including
his own two wives, and loot everything. Even David's own followers turned against him in the first moment of desperation at
this calamity, but David took refuge in his religious faith and
consulted the divine oracle through Abiathar. Instructed to pursue the Amalekites and assured of success, David and his band
set out on the expedition. Lack of food, which had been taken
by the raiders, made some of the party drop out exhausted, but
an Egyptian slave of the Amalekites gave welcome assistance and
offered to lead David to the enemy camp. The Amalekites were
totally annihilated, the women and children released, and much
more booty recovered than they themselves had lost, especially
flocks and herds.

When the returning victors came to those who had dropped

out from exhaustion, the question arose about the division of the spoil. Those who had fought sought to deny to those who had fallen by the way the right to a share. David showed his sense of justice by ruling that all should have an equal share, and thereby created a precedent which received official formulation in the priestly legal tradition (Num. 31:27-47). The story affords one example of Israelite law in the making. The law codes contained in the Pentateuch are composite documents emerging out of the traditions preserved in the various centers of worship. The religious sanctuaries were the most stable centers of a community in process of settlement; the priests thus became custodians of all law, civil and moral as well as ceremonial. Some of this law grew out of their own oracular consultations or from pronouncements of the cult prophets. Other legal rules arose from decisions of kings, elders, and military leaders like David, which established precedents for future occasions. We have here an example of the latter.

The Battle of Gilboa (31:1-13)

Meanwhile at Gilboa the battle raged between the Philistines and the Israelites led by Saul. Badly wounded and afraid that he would be treated like Samson and made an object of sport, Saul besought his armor-bearer to slay him. When the man refused, he slew himself. Jonathan and two other of Saul's sons were also slain, and the Israelites were thoroughly routed. The victorious Philistines cut off Saul's head, placed his armor in their temple, and fastened his body to the wall of Bethshan, along with the bodies of his sons; but the men of Jabesh-gilead, whose city Saul in his early days had rescued from the Ammonites, came by night, took away the bodies to Jabesh, and burned them there. Burning the dead has little precedent or parallel in Hebrew practice. The Chronicler, in his version of the incident, replaces it by burying (I Chron. 10:12). Amos declares burning the dead to be an abomination (Amos 2:1). Actually we have other cases where corpses were burned, but always they were of men cut off by God from his Covenant (Joshua 7:25; I Kings 13:2). Saul regarded himself as God-forsaken, hence his resort to the witch of Endor. It may well be that the men of Jabesh-gilead regarded his suicide as a confirmation of his divine rejection. In this case, the burning of his body would have been an acknowledgment by them of his exclusion from the covenanted life of Israel, even

though they showed their indebtedness to him by rescuing his
body from the dishonor to which the Philistines had subjected it.

DAVID AS KING

II Samuel 1:1—24:25

David at Hebron (1:1—4:12)

The Report of Saul's Death (1:1-16)

The setting of this story is the arrival of an Amalekite, against
whose tribe David had just conducted a successful expedition
(I Sam. 30). The man reported the raid of the Israelite army,
and gave a version of the death of Saul which differs from that
in I Samuel 31. According to his story, Saul, so exhausted that
he leaned upon his spear, could not escape his enemies. He
pleaded with the passing Amalekite (instead of with his armor-
bearer) to slay him. This the Amalekite did, and thus Saul did
not perish by his own hand. Because the Amalekite had lifted
his hand against the Lord's anointed king, David ordered that he
be executed by his young men.

Some interpreters find here a second version of the story
of Saul's death, but intrinsically there is nothing against the
view that both I Samuel 31 and II Samuel 1 belong to the early
tradition. One additional complication arises in II Samuel 4,
where David declares that he slew the Amalekite with his own
hand (II Sam. 4:10). It is probable that in II Samuel 1 we
have a fabrication by the Amalekite, who sought to curry favor
with David through his report, even bringing Saul's royal in-
signia, the "crown" and the "armlet," and thus flatteringly suggesting that David is now rightful king. The statement in II
Samuel 4:10 can then be understood as carelessness about detail
on David's part or as due to the tendency to take the responsibility for actions ordered of his followers.

We note that the Amalekite described himself as a kind of
"resident alien," a "sojourner." This term covered those living
in Israel's land and under Hebrew protection. Such people had
not the same rights as the Hebrews, but the various law codes
offered them certain benefits and privileges (Exod. 22:21-22;
23:9; Deut. 14:28-29; 24:14-15, 19-22). If this was the status

of the Amalekite, he was not in the raiding group and may even have been resident in Israel because of some blood feud with his own people. This would explain still more his desire to curry favor with David.

David's Lament (1:17-27)

David composed a death dirge over Saul and Jonathan. This is generally acknowledged, like the Song of Deborah (Judges 5), to be an early example of Hebrew poetry, and there is no reason not to attribute it to David. This would confirm the later tradition which regarded him as the psalmist par excellence. The poem under consideration is said to have been preserved in the "Book of Jashar" (vs. 18), which appears to have been a collection of early Hebrew poetry (see also Joshua 10:12-13). This shows that the Deuteronomic historians and editors had earlier written material on which to draw.

In the poem the victory over Israel is not to be announced in Philistia, lest the Philistine women come out in jubilant procession. Nature is bidden to withhold its blessings; even the deep, which underlies the flat disclike earth and provides its springs, is to stay its bounty, for Saul is dead and his shield lies rusting on the field of battle. David sings of the valor of Saul and Jonathan. They were father and son together in death as in life, their swords and arrows feeding on the fat and blood of those whom they slew. If the Philistine women lead in rejoicing, the Israelite women are summoned to lead in mourning. The poem finishes with special mourning for Jonathan, David's covenant-brother.

The Anointing of David at Hebron (2:1-7)

Saul's death brought division. Two rival Hebrew kingdoms arose. One under David embraced Judah and was centered at Hebron, whither David went with his wives, household, and armed men, under divine instruction, presumably secured by consulting Abiathar's oracle. The other kingdom was set up, as we shall see immediately, across Jordan, under Saul's son, Ishbosheth.

Hebron was an ancient city dating back to patriarchal days (Gen. 13:18; 23:2). Here the men of Judah assembled and anointed David as their king. David at once sought to cultivate the men of Jabesh-gilead because of their loyalty to Saul and their treatment of his dead body. There was policy in this. Such loyalty could mean much if transferred to David, and these men were in the area where Saul's followers were seeking to perpetuate his kingdom.

The Civil War with Ish-bosheth (2:8-32)

Abner, Saul's commander, was trying to establish a continuation of Saul's dynasty across Jordan at Mahanaim. He made Saul's son, Ish-bosheth, king. According to I Chronicles 8:33 and 9:39, the man's name was originally "Eshbaal" (Ish-baal), literally, "man of Baal." Thus we have a term borrowed from Canaanite fertility cults employed in a Hebrew name—a by no means uncommon practice. It shows that practices and divine titles used by the Canaanite inhabitants were taken over by the Hebrews. In Hebrew, the term "Baal" could mean "Lord" and thus it could serve as a title applied to God. Thus, the name of Eshbaal is not necessarily any indication of pagan affiliations. In the time of the eighth-century prophets, the combination of names with "Baal" came into disrepute, especially because of the spread of fertility cult rites in the worship of the Lord (Hosea 2:16). Probably for this reason the name is changed to "Ish-bosheth," which means "man of shame."

Ish-bosheth was made king over all the tribes except Judah ("Ashurites" probably refers to the Asherites), and his capital was in Gilead, a region particularly favorable to Saul's family because the late king had done so much for it (I Sam. 11). Ish-bosheth was probably a minor, since Abner seems to have assumed the powers of regent. By the pool of Gibeon, Abner and his men met Joab and David's followers, who may have been the party sent by David to Jabesh-gilead. Fighting began as a contest between twelve men from each party, but this tournament developed into a general conflict in which Abner's party was routed. Pursued by Asahel, Joab's brother, Abner fled from the field of battle. He sought to evade Asahel, fearing a blood feud with Joab should he slay his fleet-footed pursuer (vs. 22). Evasion and persuasion failing, he killed Asahel, but Joab and Abishai took up the pursuit. They followed after Abner and the Benjaminites who joined him, but at last yielded to Abner's plea and gave up the pursuit, allowing him to return with the remnants of his band across Jordan to Mahanaim. The "Arabah" is the depression of land extending from the Sea of Galilee through the Jordan Valley and the Dead Sea to the Gulf of Aqabah. Probably Joab's decision was dictated by common sense; he was far from his base and his band was weary.

This is the first important appearance of Joab, David's nephew (I Sam. 26:6; I Chron. 2:16). His dominant role in subsequent events will be seen as the story develops. He was a loyal follower whose military leadership and prowess stood David in good stead, so that Joab became an indispensable commander-in-chief.

The Treason of Abner (3:1-16)

A list of David's family is followed in verse 6 by an account of the continued conflict between David and Ish-bosheth. This story begins with the quarrel between Ish-bosheth and Abner. The latter had had relations with Rizpah, one of Saul's concubines. The wrongness of this act was not regarded as primarily a moral issue. It arose from the fact that Saul's wives and concubines passed into the possession of his successor. Abner was performing an act of insubordination, and his action could be regarded as a direct challenge to the royal rights of Ish-bosheth. Abner endeavored to evade this by seeing only the moral aspect. "Am I a dog's head?" he asked, a question which was grounded in the fact that in the Near East, the dog was a despised and impure animal. The attitude of Ish-bosheth led Abner to seek revenge by coming to terms with David. He promised to bring over all Israel to David, but the latter demanded, as a necessary precondition for any covenant with Abner, the return of Michal. There was political wisdom in this, for as Saul's son-in-law, David could have a greater claim on the loyalty of the rest of Israel. David is represented as making the request for Michal's return directly to Ish-bosheth, who complied. On her return, Michal was met by Abner, who then presumably carried out his part of the agreement with David.

Abner's Death (3:17-39)

Abner was virtually the leader of the rest of Israel, and Ish-bosheth was his puppet. In accord with his agreement with David, Abner won over all Israel to David's side, apparently with some ease. The tribe of Benjamin may have shown some reluctance, and hence it is singled out for special attention (vs. 19). It was Saul's own tribe, but Abner was also a Benjaminite and the return of Michal would help to swing things in David's favor.

Abner went to report to David at Hebron and was entertained

at a feast from which Joab was absent. Abner arranged to assemble the leaders of Israel to make a covenant with David as
their king and then departed. Joab on his return heard of the
visit and protested to David, but secretly he sent out his own
messengers to apprehend Abner and bring him back to Hebron.
Without David's knowledge, Joab slew Abner, in revenge for the
death of his brother Asahel. When the news reached David, he was
horrified at the treacherous act, partly no doubt because of the
harm it might do to the negotiations in which Abner was involved.
He invoked a curse on Joab and his house. We see the strong
sense of blood revenge in Hebrew relations in the act of Joab
and the terrible burden of bloodguilt in the horrible curse of
David. Joab's fiery temper is evident throughout this story.

Abner was given a public mourning and funeral, David being the principal mourner. Undoubtedly there was a political
motive in David's action, for he had been on the verge of gaining
the whole kingdom when this tragic act occurred. He was still
anxious to placate those who had followed Abner and who had
been about to acknowledge his own kingship. The lament of
David over Abner in verses 33-34 conveys an authentic note and
again discloses David as a poet and psalmist. In the closing
verses of the chapter the editor is careful to show that no blame
rested on the shoulders of David. David could not deal with Joab
his nephew as he dealt with other murderers, but he left him
to the judgment of God.

The Murder of Ish-bosheth (4:1-12)

Ish-bosheth's spirit was broken with the loss of Abner, who
was the dominant power of the kingdom. The story emphasizes
the fact that Ish-bosheth's murderers were Benjaminites, and thus
Saul's fellow tribesmen. It then digresses into an account of
Jonathan's son, Mephibosheth (originally Merib-baal—I Chron.
8:34—and altered for the same reason as the name of Eshbaal; see comment on 2:8-32). This digression seems to have no
bearing on the murder of Ish-bosheth; rather it explains the boy's
lameness and thus provides a background for the later events
recorded in II Samuel 9.

Confusion apparently abounded in the entourage of Ish-
bosheth, and his murderers were able to take him unaware as he
rested in the heat of the day. There seems to have been no ade-
quate bodyguard, for with Abner's death the backbone of order

was broken. The murderers brought the head of Ish-bosheth to David, reasoning that they would be credited for this deed and hoping that it would give them good standing with the one who was manifestly to be the new king. They miscalculated, however. Their attempt to represent themselves as agents of the divine judgment met with little sympathy from David who, out of his own experience of the redeeming activity of the Lord, had learned to preserve life whenever possible, even that of his enemies. Citing the precedent of his treatment of the Amalekite who had claimed credit for the slaying of Saul (see comment on 1:1-16), David now ordered his young men to kill these murderers, whose crime was more dastardly because they had taken the life of a righteous man and had done so while he slept. Probably David regarded Ish-bosheth as so weak and ineffective, now that Abner was gone, that alive he would have offered no serious obstacle to David's attaining the kingship over all Israel. David's action now publicly showed that he had had nothing to do with the murder of his ineffective rival, while his treatment of the murderers demonstrated his concern for justice. The blood of Ish-bosheth cried up to heaven for justice until those who shed it were destroyed from the earth (vs. 11; see Gen. 4:10). A life taken, it was thought, had to be avenged.

David at Jerusalem (5:1—8:18)

The King of All Israel (5:1-5)

In this brief section we have some repetition. Verses 1 and 2 represent the same event as verse 3. Verse 3 seems more authentic, since the elders of the tribes rather than all the tribes would have met David at Hebron. The early tradition did not regard David as general over all Israel under Saul but as captain of a thousand (I Sam. 18:13). The terms of the covenant agreement between David and the elders are not recorded. The chronological details are editorial but probably are as nearly accurate as we can expect for this early period.

The Capture of Jerusalem (5:6-16)

Jerusalem was a stronghold which geographically and strategically dominated both the north and the south. Its occupation

would give David a tremendous advantage, and he needed this,
since the Philistines were probably planning a fresh campaign to
prevent him from consolidating his new power. David could see
the obvious value of the city as a permanent seat of government,
and he set about securing it. The city, occupied by the Jebusites,
had been so strong that the invading Israelites had left it alone
(Joshua 15:63; Judges 1:21). Indeed, the inhabitants were so
sure of their defenses and their secure position that they taunted
David, claiming that even a defending force of the lame and the
blind could keep his army out.

The details of the capture of the stronghold are obscure and
the Hebrew text of verse 8 is particularly difficult. The confusion
appears also in Chronicles, which gives a quite different and
equally obscure account of the capture (I Chron. 11:5-6). Reading between the lines, we may presume that the invading force
used the tunnel that connected the rock of Zion with the "Virgin's
Spring" at Gihon, which provided the city's water supply. Archaeologists have discovered a vertical shaft in the rock up which
the inhabitants may have raised water from the pool below, fed
from the spring. Some daring Israelites, possibly led by Joab, may
have climbed up this shaft and taken the defenders by surprise.
Apparently the Jebusites were not destroyed but were absorbed,
like so many other Canaanites, into the Israelite stock. The Deuteronomic editor of the Book of Judges declared that the Jebusites dwelt in the midst of Israel until his own time (Judges 1:21).

David now set about building his city, starting at "the Millo."
This word means "filling" and it may represent some kind of
earthwork, although the nature of the Millo remains a matter of
speculation. Difficulty is further raised by the statement in I
Kings 11:27 that Solomon built the Millo. It is best to leave
speculation on one side at this point, and to content ourselves
with the fact that David extended and strengthened the Jebusite
city.

The reference to Hiram in verse 11 is probably anticipatory,
since this king of Tyre was not ruling at the time of the capture
of Jerusalem. Undoubtedly cultural relations with Tyre began
early, long before Hiram helped Solomon build his Temple, and
we are told elsewhere that Hiram had established friendly relations with David (I Kings 5:1). We may presume that David's
success over the Philistines would stimulate such an alliance and
that assistance with building and materials was available to David

from Tyre at an early time. David's first governmental buildings contained Phoenician features.

In verses 13-16 there is an editorial list of David's harem and family.

The End of Philistine Power (5:17-25)

Some historians would place this campaign before the capture of Jerusalem. This city is not specifically mentioned here, but it is emphasized that David was king of all Israel. It is quite possible, however, that David, knowing what he wanted, had secured Jerusalem before the Philistines were fully aware that he had become the leader of all Israel and that they were now facing a united nation. At any rate, David's increasing power presented a major threat to the Philistine control. As the Philistine host advanced, David went to "the stronghold" (vs. 17). This may refer to Jerusalem. There he inquired of the divine oracle, and received instruction to go up against the advancing enemy. It is noteworthy that the questions asked in such consultations could always receive the simple answer "yes" or "no," showing that this inquiry of the Lord was by the method of sacred lot associated with the ephod.

The Philistines gathered on the fertile plain of Rephaim near Jerusalem. In the first battle, David raided the Philistines at Baal-perazim, literally "Lord of breaking through" and probably so called from David's victory, which could be likened to the breaking forth of flood waters. If this be so, the Lord is at this stage given the title "Baal" borrowed from the local fertility cult. As we have seen (comment on 2:8-32), it was only later that the title was dropped in Hebrew religious circles, and then because of the paganization of Israelite faith and practice under the influence of the fertility rites. The Philistines had taken their gods with them into battle, as the Israelites had earlier taken the Ark, and in the rout they left these idols behind them. David carried away the images and, according to the Chronicler, burned them (I Chron. 14:12).

A renewed attack by the Philistines led to a fresh consultation of the divine oracle by David. The Lord's instruction was to attack in the rear, and the answer is stated in such a complicated form that we may presume that a cultic prophet was consulted rather than the ephod. The sound of marching in the top of the balsam trees was to be the sign for attack. Probably the idea was that the movement of the wind was the indication of the Lord's presence, since the wind was often, in early days, identified with God's Spirit. This time the Philistines were thoroughly defeated.

The Ark at Jerusalem (6:1-23)

The last mention of the Ark was in I Samuel 7:2, where it was said to be left at Kiriath-jearim. Its fate in the interval is unknown. It had been the divine rallying center for the northern group of tribes at the sanctuaries at Shechem and Shiloh and had been the symbol of God's presence in their midst, his visible throne (vs. 2). If Jerusalem was to be truly David's capital, it must be so religiously as well as politically, and placing the Ark there would attract the northern tribes religiously to the new capital to a degree that no other means could accomplish. So the symbol for the unity of the northern tribes, with its religious implications, became a symbol for the unity of the nation as a whole. The ancient and sacred chest gave to the new capital a religious sanction.

Attended by a chosen band of warriors, David went to Baal-judah, probably another name for Kiriath-jearim (Joshua 15:9-10), where the Ark had been left. It was placed on a new cart, drawn by oxen and driven by Uzzah and his brother (see margin), the sons of Abinadab, at whose house the Ark had been kept. The Ark was brought back with music and rejoicing. At the threshing floor of Nacon, the oxen stumbled and Uzzah did something to steady the Ark, perhaps involuntarily. Exactly what he did the Hebrew text does not make clear, but the sequel is clear—Uzzah died. Remembering the early Hebrew understanding of holiness as a quasi-physical quality which pervaded all objects and persons associated with the Deity, an idea the Hebrews shared with many other peoples, we can understand that Uzzah may have been paralyzed and even struck dead by the fear aroused when he touched the holy object. Similar reactions still occur today among primitive peoples and are exploited by witch doctors. Such seems the best explanation.

David shared in the primitive reaction to the presence of a divine quality in holy objects and was unwilling to proceed further with the transportation of the Ark, so it was left at the house of Obed-edom the Gittite, presumably a Philistine resident alien. After three months, the manifest blessing attending Obed-edom was regarded as a sign that the divine wrath had abated, therefore the Ark was taken on to Jerusalem. As it moved forward, David, wearing the linen ephod—the priestly garb in this case and not the oracle (see comment on I Sam. 2:18)— sacrificed and danced before the Lord. That he should perform priestly functions and wear priestly dress is a reminder that these functions were not confined to the priestly caste as such, their chief task in early days being to consult the oracle rather than to sacrifice. It is also an indication that the king was regarded as a holy person. On arrival at Jerusalem, the Ark was housed in a tent, possibly a replica of the wilderness Tabernacle, and a series of offerings was made, culminating in a sacrificial meal. The burnt offerings were wholly offered to the Lord, but the peace offerings were communion offerings in which the broiled flesh of the sacrificial victims was shared amongst the worshipers, the blood alone being offered to God. Thus, through the life of a third party, that of the slaughtered beast, the worshipers communed with one another and with God.

David's dancing, stimulated doubtless by his religious zeal, aroused the scorn of Michal. Her ironic greeting was parried by a contemptuous reply and by a permanent estrangement which meant that the house of Saul was not continued through the house of David.

The Hopes of David and Nathan's Prophecy (7:1-17)

Most commentators regard this section as generally late. It was certainly not in the "court history," from which most of II Samuel was taken, but it does embody early material, as we shall see.

David has built himself a house of cedar and has become conscience-stricken because the Ark of the Lord is still housed only in a tent. He consults his prophet Nathan, who at first declares that the Lord is behind David's desire to build a temple. Then the prophet has a change of mind and advises against it. The implication of this change of mind is that Nathan had at first misunderstood God's will, an interesting insight into the nature of prophetic inspiration.

Nathan's speech, which follows, has two elements in it. The first is the declaration that God needs no house to dwell in, but rather sets his presence in the midst of his people wherever they are. The implication is that God's true dwelling place is the people he is shaping for himself, a teaching brought out fully in the New Testament and fulfilled in the Person of our Lord and in his Church. The second element is the promise that David's seed shall be assured of his throne forever. In these words an eternal Covenant is declared between the Lord and the house of David, whereby God's steadfast love will not be withdrawn from David's descendants, even though some will be chastened for their iniquity. David's throne shall be established forever. In verse 11 the writer plays on the double meaning of the word "house," which can mean "dynasty" as well as "dwelling place." It is not for David to build a dwelling place for God but to let God build a dynasty for him. The theme of the eternal Covenant with David is developed in Psalm 89, which many hold to be related in some way to the passage under discussion. It is in this promise of an eternal Covenant with David's seed that the Messianic hope is grounded. Running throughout Old Testament prophecy, the hope is seen in the New Testament to be fulfilled in the eternal King, Jesus, great David's greater Son.

We may assume that, in its root, the prophecy of an eternal Covenant with the house of David goes back to an early time, and this may be borne out by the fact that parts of verses 8, 9, 10, 12, 14-16 are poetic in form, whereas the rest of Nathan's prophecy is in late and inferior prose. The poetic parts of the speech may go back to some original prophetic oracle about David's house, which was utilized by the writer of chapter 7.

Into the theme so far developed verse 13 introduces a different note, for the God who declares that he does not and will not live in the earthly house here promises that David's son shall build a house for his name. This verse may be the work of the Deuteronomic editor, who was especially concerned with the centrality of the Temple in Hebrew life, as the place where God had chosen to put his name (Deut. 12:5). By this interpretation he endeavored to take the sting out of the attack on the idea of the Temple with which Nathan's prophecy begins. The best commentary on this interpretation and one in keeping with the general spirit of this speech, as outlined earlier, is contained in Acts 7:47-48: "But it was Solomon who built a house for him. Yet the Most High does not dwell in houses made with hands."

David's Prayer (7:18-29)

We come now to a kind of prose psalm. David went in and "sat before the LORD"; that is, he went into the Tent and pre-

sumably knelt before the Ark on which God's Presence was en-
throned. The prayer plays upon the key theme already introduced in Nathan's speech—the dual meaning of "house," taking
it in its second sense of "dynasty." It is interesting to note a
parallel to this usage in Exodus 1:21, where God rewards the
faithful midwives as he "built them houses"—the literal meaning of "gave them families"—in which their name should live
on. The prayer celebrates the Lord's greatness and uniqueness.
Israel, too, is unique, like no other nation, for God has freely
chosen it, binding it to himself by moral ties and performing his
mighty acts on its behalf. Other nations may be bound to their
gods by quasi-physical ties which make them mutually necessary
to one another, but God and Israel have no such bond (vs. 23).
The key to Israel's existence as a nation was not that it was in
some mythical way physically descended from a god, but that it
had been elected, delivered from Egypt, and brought into Canaan
by the Lord's free activity. The prayer describes this election of
Israel as God's "making himself a name." Israel has no merit in
itself by which to lay claim on God's choice. The whole matter
lies in the inscrutability of God's purpose and manifests his grace
and glory. Before the greatness of such a God, shown in this final
act of grace, Israel must walk humbly, and if Israel, then David
too, who likewise owes all he is and has to God and to no virtue
he himself possesses. The Lord has freely established Israel to be
his people forever (vs. 24), and now he has promised to establish
David and his seed forever on the throne of Israel. David prays
that God, whose words are faithful, will fulfill his promise. What
God has commenced, he will carry through. He cannot belie himself.

A Summary of David's Wars (8:1-18)

This summary is provided by the Deuteronomic editor. It records David's conquests over the Philistines and the Moabites,
from whom he exacted tribute and two-thirds of whose population was placed under the ban and put to death. Presumably the
reference here is to the male population. No reason is given for
this ban.

Hadadezer, king of Zobah, ruled over a small state near Damascus. Apparently he got into trouble with David by going to
the assistance of the Ammonites against him (see II Sam. 10:6).
As a result, David captured a large number of fighting men and

enough chariot horses to serve his own military and domestic pur-
poses. The figures are probably exaggerated. This campaign drew
in the Syrians around Damascus, who in turn were subjugated.
David returned with much booty, including the gold shields used
by Hadadezer's soldiers.

This victory also brought other consequences, for the king of
Hamath sent congratulations and gifts, the latter being consecrated by David to the service of the Lord.

The other triumph recorded is that over the Edomites, as a consequence of which Edom became a tributary state and garrisons
of Israelite troops were established throughout its territory.

The chapter finishes by praising the justice and equity of
David's rule and by furnishing a list of his chief officials. There
are errors in the text. The origin and family of Zadok are obscure.
Ahitub was the father of Abimelech and a descendant of Eli (I
Sam. 14:3), so that we should read: "Abiathar the son of
Abimelech the son of Ahitub, and Zadok." Zadok, according to
the most acceptable theory, was the chief priest of the Jebusite
sanctuary at Jerusalem. Benaiah had charge of the foreign mercenaries, "the Cherethites and the Pelethites," probably Phoenicians.

The Personal Affairs of David (9:1—12:31)

David's Kindness to Mephibosheth (9:1-13)

It was customary in the ancient Near East for a new dynastic
ruler to put to death all the descendants of the preceding royal line
and thus eliminate possible rivals. Jonathan's son Merib-baal (a
name later altered to "Mephibosheth"; see comment on II Sam.
2:8-32 and 4:1-12) was exactly in this position—a potential rival.
He had been living at Lo-debar near Mahanaim and thus in proximity to his uncle Ish-bosheth. At the time of the incident recorded here he was apparently the only descendant of Saul left
alive. This would mean that this occurrence must be subsequent
to that recorded in II Samuel 21, when Saul's sons were killed to
satisfy the Gibeonites. Probably Mephibosheth went into hiding
because of his lameness, a condition already explained in II Samuel 4:4. David remembered his covenant with Jonathan and his
promise to Saul. His inquiry whether there was any descendant of
Saul left to whom he could show covenant mercy ("kindness")
brought to light the existence of Mephibosheth. The latter was

brought to David, who endeavored to make amends for his for-
getfulness of covenant obligation. Mephibosheth was set up in a
house; Saul's servant, Ziba, was made his steward; he was granted
the signal honor of being a regular guest at the royal table; and all
the income of the estates of Saul and his house was given to him.

The story is an interesting commentary on the strength of the
covenant bond and also on the character of David. Doubtless it
would help David politically with factions still attached to Saul's
family, if he treated Saul's grandson well. But there is something
deeper implied in this story; David at this point was a man of integrity who was prepared to accept his covenant obligations fully
and who sought to show covenant love, steadfast loyalty, within
his covenant bond.

The Conflict with the Ammonites (10:1-19)

The Ammonites under Nahash had earlier been in trouble with
Saul (I Sam. 11), but apparently Nahash had maintained friendly
relations with David, since David could state that Nahash had
"dealt loyally" with him. At Nahash's death, David sought to
perpetuate this state of affairs with Hanun, the son of Nahash.
The term translated "dealt loyally" is a covenant term, possibly
implying the existence of some kind of treaty or covenant bond.
David sent emissaries to express his condolence, but the counselors
of Hanun, perhaps in the light of Israel's recent victories over
other peoples, advised against a favorable reception of the envoys,
arguing that they were spies. Hanun's treatment of David's messengers was a complete breach of political etiquette even in those
days, since such political emissaries were sacrosanct. He made the
offense worse by the mode of his treatment, for shaving off part
of their beard and mutilating their garments humiliated the
men and made them objects of ridicule. The beard was a symbol
of honor; hence the men "were greatly ashamed." The treatment
had as its design a symbolic humiliation of David and his people.

David sent Joab and his armed host against an augmented
army, for the Ammonites in anticipation of trouble had hired
various Syrian groups as mercenaries. The Ammonites drew up in
front of their city gate, and the Syrian forces assembled in the
open country. By a strategic maneuver, Joab attacked and routed
the Syrians, using a picked force out of his armed host. With the
Syrians routed, the Ammonites took to flight, and Joab returned
to Jerusalem.

The Syrians gathered themselves together again, however, and tried to avenge their defeat. Under the leadership of Hadadezer of Zobah and his army commander, Shobach, they assembled across Jordan at Helam, only to be routed once more, this time decisively. In consequence they made peace, entered into a covenant with David, and became tributary to Israel. The Ammonites continued to give trouble.

Bathsheba (11:1-27)

David had in his army a high-ranking mercenary soldier from the Hittite people named Uriah, with a Hebrew wife named Bathsheba. We may presume that Uriah's home was a typical Eastern house with open courtyard, and that it was sufficiently near the ridge on which David's palace was built for the king to overlook it. In any case, David developed a passion for Bathsheba which led to adultery. When Bathsheba conceived, David sought for a means to evade the consequences of his crime. He summoned Uriah home from the campaign against Ammon on the pretense of seeking news about the fighting, and offered him a night at home. Uriah, true to the warrior's oath to abstain from sexual intercourse in time of battle, slept at the door of the king's house and did not visit his home. Having failed in this first attempt, David sought to make Uriah drunk, but again he failed to accomplish his purpose. Uriah was sent back to Joab, bearing a letter which instructed the general to set Uriah in the center of the fighting. This ruse succeeded. Uriah was slain and David married Bathsheba, who bore him a son.

This story has little if anything to redeem it. It shows David in an evil light. The consequences of his sin bore down upon him all his days, as the subsequent story of his life discloses. He at least had enough sense of responsibility to marry Bathsheba. Through the story Uriah stands out as a man of loyalty, who remained true to his warrior's oath. His nobility of character shows up David's sin all the more. The remaining years of David's life are a reminder that the judgment of God on sin cannot be avoided even by his "anointed." The wrath of God is revealed from heaven against all ungodliness and unrighteousness of men.

Nathan and David's Sin (12:1-31)

Nathan belongs in the great prophetic succession, with his deep spiritual insight and keen understanding of the divine intention and purpose. It was he who withstood David and brought home to him the reality of his sin. Like those of the later canonical prophets, Nathan's messages seem to have come through creative imagination and vision rather than ecstatic emotional upsurge. He attracted the king's interest and got his message across to him by a shrewd use of imagination. The king, the final court of appeal in matters of justice, would not fail to respond to the story of the poor man and his one ewe lamb. As David rose to the bait and declared that the offender deserved to perish and that, according to the legal ruling, he must restore the lamb fourfold (Exod. 22:1), the prophet delivered the shrewd counterthrust which drove the meaning of the parable home to the king's conscience. By legal right he had appropriated the harem of his predecessor Saul. God had given him much, but he had set his wolfish eyes upon the wife of one of his own trusted officers and had smitten the husband with the sword. In measured terms Nathan pronounced the judgment of God on David's sin, foretelling strife, division, and infidelity in the royal household to such a degree that, unlike David's secret sin with Bathsheba, these tragedies would be manifest to all Israel. David was stirred to such penitence that God's forgiveness was assured, but the punishment had still to be borne. Part of the price he would pay was that the child of his and Bathsheba's sin must die.

This is a remarkable illustration of the heights which the prophetic ministry could attain in early days. Elijah's fiery denunciations of Ahab (I Kings 21:17-24), set alongside the shrewd and indirect approach of Nathan to David, remind us of how varied the prophetic method could be in those days, as preaching can be now. The parable of the ewe lamb was beautifully conceived and delivered, shaped to its purpose of awakening David's interest and piercing his conscience.

The last part of this section shows us the judgment of God working out. David might have silenced Nathan by decreeing his death, but even the king of Israel acknowledged himself to be under God's word. The king was appointed and anointed by the Lord, and neither David nor his successors laid claim to a divine nature or other than a divinely delegated authority. It was this theocratic understanding of kingship which meant that the king, like the commonest of his subjects, must stand before the bar of God and listen humbly to his prophets.

David, stricken with penitence, still sought by prayer and fasting to divert the judgment of God. But judgment descended, and the child died. David showed his greatness in the way he bore his punishment and retained his faith. Even God's forgiveness does not mean that we shall escape all the consequences of sin, but if we are in God's forgiveness, he gives us grace to bear them and to bear them as a testimony to our faith. This happened to David. Out of his grief, he arose, went to the sanctuary, and worshiped.

David's saying about the dead child in verse 23 is rooted in the common conception of Sheol, the place of the departed. His words imply that the child had passed from all that was worth while to something that was little better than nonexistence. From Sheol there was no return, so David could find no hope at this point. He, too, could go to Sheol by death, but it would be no place of joyful reunion; rather it was a place where he, too, would be absorbed into the meaningless existence which had overtaken his child. It is against such a background that we must understand the growing hope in the Old Testament of a resurrection from the dead and grasp the full significance of our Lord's triumph, in which he abolished death and brought life and immortality to light (II Tim. 1:10). The men of Old Testament times walked in the land of the shadow of death and waited for the light to shine upon them.

Later Solomon was born to Bathsheba, his birth being interpreted as a divine gift. The chapter closes with an account of a further attack by Joab on the Ammonites in their walled city of Rabbah. The final credit for taking this city was left by Joab for David himself. The city was captured, the Ammonite crown of gold was added to David's regalia, and he returned from battle with great spoil. The Ammonites were generally subjugated and apparently were turned into industrial slaves for Israel.

The Tragedy of David's Family (13:1—20:26)

We come now to a section of the Book of Samuel which revolves around the figure of Absalom. Here is a very human, intimate, and unvarnished account of David's family. It is arranged immediately after the Bathsheba episode, as if it, too, should be regarded as part of the divine judgment, even though the preceding section seems to suggest that because of David's repentance the death of the child was sufficient punishment.

Amnon and Tamar (13:1-22)

Tamar was the full sister of Absalom, but only the half-sister of Amnon. Marriage between half-brother and sister was apparently countenanced in the early days, as the case of Abraham and Sarah shows (Gen. 20:11-13); it was not forbidden until the Priestly Code (Lev. 18:9), which embodies late legal tradition. Amnon's desire for Tamar must not be regarded therefore as wrong according to the standards of that day. His crime lay in forcing her and then in refusing to accept responsibility for his crime by marrying her. Tamar's plea that such a thing was not done in Israel was an appeal to the moral custom rather than to some fixed law of the time. Such conduct was universally regarded as wrong in Israel. Having had his will of Tamar, Amnon's consuming passion for her turned into a violent hate, a transformation of feeling often illustrated in literature and in the casebooks of psychology. Love and hatred are rooted close together in the human heart. Amnon's loathing of himself because of his deed was projected on the victim of his lust.

Absalom's hot anger was stirred by the deed, but he bided his time. In the meantime he took the wronged Tamar into his home. David was angry but spared Amnon, presumably, as the Greek text adds, because he was his first-born.

Absalom's Flight (13:23-39)

At last Absalom's opportunity came. The time of sheepshearing was also a time of religious festival (I Sam. 25). Absalom, responsible for the sheepshearing, arranged for a feast to which he invited his father, David. The king refused, and countered the request for the presence of Amnon, as if he had his suspicions of Absalom's motive. The request for Amnon's presence could be justified, however, since as eldest son he would represent David. Absalom showed in this story a capacity for silent hate and shrewd cunning which characterized him throughout later events. His importunity overcame David's reluctance. Amnon was allowed to attend the feast, along with the king's other sons. Once Amnon was in his hands, Absalom carried his plan to completion. Amnon was murdered, and the other sons fled, possibly because they suspected that Absalom was now determined to secure for himself the succession and might remove potential rivals. Rumor spread and reached David that all his sons were slain, but his nephew,

Jonadab, shrewdly guessed at the truth that only Amnon had been slain because of his treatment of Absalom's sister. The appearance of the other sons confirmed his surmise, and a royal mourning for Amnon ensued.

Meantime Absalom fled to the Geshurites. David, comforted about Amnon and fond of his erring son, longed for Absalom's return.

Absalom's Return (14:1-33)

Joab divined the state of David's mind and with the help of a wise woman from Tekoa devised a stratagem. We have here the first appearance of a group which, by Jeremiah's time, had become a professional class ranking alongside the prophets and the priests (Jer. 18:18). These people, "the wise," were nearer the common folk than the other two classes. Most of them were men. They were noted for their practical shrewdness, which was regarded as a divine gift. Resort was made to them for counsel in the practical details of life, and they appear to have assembled a body of shrewd wisdom noted for its utilitarian flavor and enshrined in our Bible, especially in the Book of Proverbs. Never possessing the authority of the priests and the prophets, the word of "the wise" nevertheless was thought to have a divine quality. In David's reign this group began to gain prominence (see later II Samuel 16:23; 20:16-22).

Joab and the wise woman planned a dramatic approach to David. The woman went to David, disguised as a widow in mourning and pleading a case which she could rightfully take to the supreme court of appeal. In a parabolic presentation, of which later wisdom was fond, she told of two sons who had quarreled, one killing the other and thereby according to law forfeiting his own life also. But if the remaining son were killed for his crime, she would be left destitute and the family name would be wiped out. The significance of the latter plea lies in the fact that men could live on only in their posterity. If both sons perished, then her husband's "name," a word equivalent in Hebrew thought to "personal substance," would have no extension down through time in his descendants. In the plea there is also the implication that other members of the family were anxious to see the law of retribution carried out in order that the inheritance might pass to them.

As with Nathan, so here. David finally gave a judgment that

stayed the hand of the avenger of blood and suspended the opera-
tion of retributive justice in the case of the son. The woman then
turned the parable on David himself. It was his sons who had
quarreled, and, by his judgment, the king was convicting himself.
He ought to call home the son he had banished, for in banishing
Absalom he was depriving the Israelite people of its royal heir.
Once more the speech reverts to the Hebrew view of the nature of
death. Dying is like water spilt on the ground. Life is dissipated.
That had been the fate of Amnon. In bringing back Absalom,
David would be serving God. The extent of the Lord's jurisdiction
explains this reference. Absalom in banishment would no longer
serve the God of Israel as he ought. He was an outcast, not only
from his own land but also from the worship of the Lord. At the
end of this appeal, the woman protected herself by returning to
her own parabolic case and by speaking as if it were actuality.

David guessed that Joab was behind the plea, and when this was
confirmed by the wise woman, he agreed to allow Absalom to return. Joab received instructions to bring back Absalom, although
the latter was not to be allowed in David's presence.

There is a digression dealing with Absalom's striking appearance and including a description of Absalom's family.

Two years after his return to Jerusalem, Absalom resolved to
seek David's presence. After his summons to Joab for help had
failed twice, he set Joab's barley field on fire. This soon brought
results, and Joab told the king, who summoned Absalom. David
was apparently reconciled to his son, although Absalom's attitude
remains open to question.

Absalom's Conspiracy (15:1-12)

Absalom now entered into a deeper intrigue against his father.
David was aging and his prestige had been damaged by the affair
with Bathsheba. Absalom therefore sought to ingratiate himself
with his father's subjects. He stood at the king's palace and talked
to all who came on business, sympathizing with those who had
come for a royal judgment on some grievance, showing an apparent interest in the private life of the litigant, and implying that
he himself could give a better judgment than the king as the present government was incompetent. By his charm and sympathy,
Absalom began to command a following. He also built up his position by gathering a bodyguard of fifty men and driving around in
a chariot, thus advertising himself as a claimant for the royal suc-

cession. Since no precedent had yet been established with regard
to the matter, he could not reckon on any law of primogeniture.

After four years, Absalom felt strong enough to make an attempt for the throne. He sought permission from David to keep
a vow in Hebron, a strange place to worship the Lord since Jerusalem was, with the presence of the Ark, now the established center of religious practice. There was policy, however, in this choice
of a center, for it had been David's old capital and was the rallying center for the tribe of Judah. It seems highly probable that
Absalom was playing upon some dissatisfaction in the latter tribe
at the transfer of the capital to Jerusalem. At Hebron, Absalom
gathered his followers together. He was joined by Ahithophel,
Bathsheba's grandfather (compare II Sam. 11:3 with 23:34),
who had been David's counselor, possibly a "wise man," who may
have joined Absalom because of the dishonor brought on Bathsheba. The plans were well laid. Key persons in all the cities were
kept in readiness to announce Absalom's kingship at the appropriate signal, and Absalom seems to have obtained a large and growing following.

David's Flight (15:13-29)

Capitalizing on the many grievances throughout David's kingdom, Absalom had already achieved some success. David, taken
by surprise, fled his capital accompanied by his ministers and protected by his bodyguard of mercenaries, including Philistines from
Gath. Among the latter was a recently joined soldier of fortune,
Ittai, who appears to have been the leader of the Gittites, since he
was bidden return and take them with him. If so, the Gittites were
as a whole a recent addition to the bodyguard. Despite the absence
of long attachment and obligation to David, Ittai elected to stay
with the king, undoubtedly attracted by the same personal qualities which had established David among his people. The priests
Abiathar and Zadok accompanied David with the Ark, but David
refused to allow it to leave the city, electing that Jerusalem should
remain the center of God's presence among his people. If God
were not favorable to him, the presence of the Ark in his fleeing
band would make no difference. He would put his trust in God's
faithfulness and rely on no talisman to help him win his battles.
The priests were therefore ordered to remain in Jerusalem, with
the added instruction that they were to act as spies. Meanwhile
David retreated in grief.

Hushai the Archite (15:30-37)

David proceeded up the steep ascent of the Mount of Olives, past the high place, his head covered and his feet bare as outward signs of his grief. News that his counselor, Ahithophel, had joined Absalom served but to increase David's grief and drew forth the prayer that he should give the pretender bad counsel. Hushai the Archite came almost as an answer to the prayer. In verse 37 he is termed David's "friend." This may have been an official title, and Hushai, a Gentile, may have belonged to a special group of courtiers who served as David's companions or "friends." David sent him back to Jerusalem, with instructions to offer his services to Absalom and so to act as a spy within the center of the enemy camp, using the priests Zadok and Abiathar to transmit his messages to David.

Ziba's Deceit (16:1-4)

Mephibosheth's servant, Ziba, joined David, bringing supplies of food and wine for the refugees. When asked why his master had not accompanied him, Ziba deceitfully implied that Mephibosheth hoped that in the political turmoil he would himself be given his father's throne, whereupon David gave to the servant all Mephibosheth's possessions. This hasty act, performed without any attempt to hear the other side of the story, does not show the king in a good light. In the sequel, Mephibosheth gave Ziba the lie and showed his loyalty to David (II Sam. 19:25-27).

Shimei's Cursing (16:5-14)

Saul's fellow tribesmen in Benjamin had continued to harbor resentment against David. Shimei, one of Saul's relatives, cursed David in no uncertain terms as he passed Bahurim, a place once associated with Michal (II Sam. 3:16). Being pelted with stones and being cursed as a man of blood were accepted by David with complete restraint. He would not let his bodyguard deal with Shimei, for he saw that in some sense even this was within the judgment of God on him. He could not keep the love and respect of his son, so he had no right to expect the respect of one of Saul's family. Perhaps God would somehow put matters right if he endured this new indignity in the right spirit.

Ahithophel and Hushai (16:15—17:14)

Meantime Hushai the Archite had arrived at Absalom's head-quarters and offered his services to Absalom, who knew him to be David's friend. The latter fact cast doubts on Hushai's sincerity, for friendship meant covenant and Hushai was apparently breaking with his steadfast covenant love to David. Hence the question, "Is this your loyalty [covenant love] to your friend?" Hushai's flattering reply apparently reassured Absalom.

The pretender now sought advice from Ahithophel. The latter advised that David be dishonored. Absalom was to show that he had assumed the kingship by appropriating that part of the royal harem which had been left in Jerusalem. We have to remember that every new monarch took over by right his predecessor's harem. Absalom's act would make the breach between himself and David final. He pitched a wedding tent on the roof of the palace and publicly manifested his possession of his father's harem. The advice of Ahithophel, the wise man, is compared at this point to the oracular advice of seer or priest, so perceptive was it assumed to be.

Ahithophel further advised Absalom to gather an army speedily and pursue David, arguing that the king could then be overtaken and slain while he was weary and discouraged. Absalom, however, was suspicious of this sound advice and turned to Hushai, who had been sent by David with the very purpose of upsetting the plans of the rebels. Hushai countered Ahithophel's advice of speedy pursuit by emphasizing David's experience in campaigning. His bodyguard was so trained that Absalom could not expect to catch David napping. Rather his own untrained men would likely be caught in a trap and a great slaughter would ensue, the effect of which would be bad on the morale of his followers. Hushai therefore counseled that time be taken to gather an army from all Israel, large enough to ensure victory. Only superior numbers could defeat the experienced troops of David. Absalom was immediately convinced, and Hushai's ruse succeeded. The narrator sees a divine overruling here in the fact that Absalom ignored Ahithophel's good advice (vs. 14).

David Crosses the Jordan (17:15-29)

Hushai hastened to get word to David concerning his counsel to Absalom. Through the priests he advised David to cross the

River Jordan. David apparently had a system of relays whereby the messages from Jerusalem could reach him. Unfortunately the presence of David's couriers at En-rogel was reported to Absalom by a lad, and they were compelled to take refuge in the well of a house in Bahurim which, in spite of Shimei, appears to have had also some inhabitants friendly to David's cause. Absalom's servants, hot in pursuit of the messengers, were misdirected by the woman of the house, and the couriers made their way to David, who by daybreak had crossed Jordan with all his party.

Ahithophel, finding his advice rejected, was shrewd enough to see that David now had the advantage and thus to read his own doom, knowing how David would deal with a treacherous counselor. He went home and hanged himself.

David was now established across Jordan around the old center of Mahanaim, with Joab commanding his army. Absalom, with his headquarters at Jerusalem, had given the command of his army to Amasa, whose family tree seems mysteriously involved, for it relates him both to the Ammonites through Nahash and to Joab through Zeruiah (vss. 25 and 27). The battle line was formed in Gilead, David's army being well provisioned by tried and trusted friends. This was the area in which Ish-bosheth had set up his kingdom, and it is a testimony to David's personality and attractiveness that he should have such support. Of significance, too, is the fact that help came from the Ammonites against whom he had campaigned.

Absalom's Death (18:1-18)

David organized his army and marched it out in three divisions, led respectively by Joab, Abishai (Joab's brother), and Ittai the Gittite. The king himself, against his own desire but under strong pressure from his followers, remained behind in Mahanaim. Before they left, he ordered his commanders to deal gently with Absalom. A great battle ensued in the forest of Ephraim, an area west of Jordan difficult to locate today. Absalom's army was routed with a great slaughter, and the forest with its rocky terrain and pitfalls helped to destroy the fleeing host.

Absalom, in flight, was caught by the head in the forked branch of an oak and left hanging, as his mule rushed on from under him. His hair is not mentioned and thus there is no ground for the traditional explanation that he was caught by his long hair. When the matter was reported to Joab, he slew Absalom with his own hand, in spite of his informant's reminder of David's injunction. The body was cast into a pit and stones were heaped on it. This was Absalom's grave, in contrast to the elaborate tomb which he had constructed for himself in the King's Valley.

David's Grief (18:19-33)

Two runners brought the news to David. Ahima-az had asked for the privilege but was refused by Joab, who sent a Cushite (an Ethiopian) instead, probably because he felt a foreigner could better convey the bad news of Absalom's death. This seems indicated by the fact that later the sight of Ahima-az, a trusty follower, bringing news is interpreted by David as a good omen (vs. 27). Joab subsequently relented and let Ahima-az go also. The latter had been David's courier earlier, and his anxiety to be the messenger may have been due either to the desire for personal advancement or, more likely, to concern for David and the desire to break gently the news of Absalom's death. Whatever the cause, he outstripped the Ethiopian and arrived first, but then his heart failed him and he simply reported a victory by the king's forces, pretending to know nothing of Absalom's fate. The arrival of the Cushite brought the truth into the open, and David was prostrated with grief.

The Return to Jerusalem (19:1-43)

Joab brought David to his senses. David was placing his personal grief before the welfare of God's people, Israel. Uppermost was his feeling as father, not his position as king. Dire rebellion had been suppressed at terrible cost to him as father, but he was also responsible for the well-being of his people, and for them the death of Absalom had been deliverance. Joab had recognized that so long as Absalom was alive the combination of cunning and ambition in his personality spelled disaster for Israel. David must decide against personal grief, however much his closest followers might sympathize with him as a father. Those who had proved their loyalty to him at personal cost were surely more deserving of his love than this son who had possessed no loyalty but had planned his father's downfall. In a very real sense, David's grief was an affront to their faithfulness. Joab's reproof was in the rough and ready speech of a soldier, but it had its effect. David suppressed his grief, and showed himself to his people.

Now came the return to Jerusalem. Confusion reigned throughout the land. Absalom was dead and David was across Jordan. There was a general feeling that David should return, but the tribe of Judah held back its support, doubtless because it had been foremost in support of Absalom. The priests were commissioned to use their services with the elders of Judah, for David would not return to Jerusalem unless the people actually invited him. The invitation came, and the king started out, the men of Judah coming to Gilgal to meet him at the crossing of the Jordan.

One by one the rebels submitted to him and joined the triumphal procession back to Jerusalem. Shimei the Benjaminite, who had cursed him, representatives from Benjamin, and Ziba the servant of Mephibosheth—all helped him and his household across the ford of Jordan. Shimei sought pardon and obtained it, even though Abishai was against such royal clemency. Mephibosheth arrived in a sorry and unkempt state, obviously having mourned since David left Jerusalem. Ziba's deceit was now uncovered, and David learned that Mephibosheth, crippled though he was, had sought to ride with him on an ass but had been hindered by Ziba. David apparently remained noncommittal. Mephibosheth and Ziba must divide the estate between them. Mephibosheth, however, declared himself content even though he lost all, so long as the king returned.

Barzillai the Gileadite, who had befriended David in Transjordan, accompanied the king to the River Jordan. David sought to take him on to Jerusalem and to reward him for his help, but the old man of fourscore years gently refused. He would return to his old and well-loved haunts, but Chimham was to accompany David in his stead and enjoy the reward.

The men of Judah, although they had gathered around Absalom, sought the center of the stage in David's return. They hurriedly brought back David across Jordan and made the loyal people of the north, the "men of Israel," jealous. A bitter verbal battle between north and south ensued, an ill omen for the days ahead when the kingdom was to be divided. The seeds of the later division are here shown to lie far back in history.

The Revolt of Sheba (20:1-26)

The quarrel between Judah and Israel flared into open revolt under the leadership of Sheba, another Benjaminite. David took into his confidence Amasa, the commander-in-chief of Absalom's rebel force and gave him charge of the men of Judah with in-

structions to pursue Sheba and the men of Israel who had originally gathered to greet David at the crossing of Jordan. Joab was
ignored, perhaps because of David's lingering resentment over
Absalom's death. In any case, Joab and Abishai soon stepped in
along with David's mercenary soldiers, for Amasa, either by intention or by nature, had proved dilatory in his pursuit of Sheba.
Joab treacherously slew Amasa, took up the pursuit vigorously,
and besieged Sheba in the city of Abel of Beth-maacah. Once
more a wise woman intervened, conferring with Joab from the
wall of the city and promising the head of Sheba if the city could
go free. The inhabitants themselves, who presumably had been
put into a false position by Sheba, executed the rebel and threw
his head from the city walls to Joab; the siege was raised and the
revolt was broken.

The text of verse 18 is obscure. The Greek translation reads:
"Let them ask in Abel and in Dan whether that had ever come to
an end which the faithful of Israel had established." The implication seems to be that Abel was faithful to the national tradition
and its judgment could be trusted.

There is a brief list of David's officers in Jerusalem appended
to the end of this section. We note that David introduced a system
of forced labor, a system greatly developed by Solomon and causing much trouble in Israel.

Miscellaneous Data: An Appendix (21:1—24:25)

The Famine and the Gibeonites (21:1-14)

A prolonged and severe famine led David to perform one of his
most tragic acts. Apparently he consulted the oracle to learn the
cause of the famine and was advised that guilt still rested upon
the nation because of Saul's massacre of the Gibeonites. The
Gibeonites were a people indigenous to Canaan, a remnant of
the original inhabitants. Saul had slain some of them, despite
the oath of the Israelites to spare them. We have no other account of this slaughter. The Gibeonites were asked to name com-
pensation, and they demanded, not money, or the death of any
man in Israel, but the hanging of seven of Saul's descendants. It
was thought that a blood curse could be removed only by the
shed blood of the man who had shed the blood originally. David
delivered up seven descendants of Saul, but, because of his cove-

nant with Jonathan, spared Jonathan's son Mephibosheth. Among those whom the Gibeonites hanged were Saul's two sons by Rizpah. She watched by the exposed bodies of the seven victims to keep off the wild beasts and birds of prey. Informed of what she had done, David had the bones buried with the bones of Saul and Jonathan in Zela of Benjamin, the burying place of Saul's family. The bones of Saul and Jonathan were removed from Jabesh-gilead, whose men had rescued them from the Philistines and respectfully cared for them.

These events must have happened prior to the story of Mephibosheth recorded earlier, since he is described there as Saul's sole descendant. This story of revenge has no justification before the living God. It can be accepted only as conforming to the custom of the time.

The Prowess of David's Heroes (21:15-22)

In a brief section we are told of David's heroes in the war with the Philistines. The emphasis falls on individuals and their prowess, not on campaigns. One interesting variation causes controversy. We are told that Goliath of Gath was slain by Elhanan (vs. 19). Some students have suggested that this is historical and that David slew a nameless giant, the name "Goliath" slipping into the David story by editorial interpolation.

David's Psalm of Victory (22:1-51)

This psalm is almost identical with Psalm 18, and in its present form can hardly be ascribed to David. It may be divided into five sections.

Verses 2-4: Faith and confidence are expressed in the Lord as the warrior God who supports, sustains, protects, and delivers those who call on him. The figures used to describe God's activity are culled from military vocabulary.

Verses 5-20: We have a representation of God as delivering men from encompassing disaster. The picture of a violent flood, as the deeps are unleashed, is paralleled by the suggestion that the subterranean cavern of Sheol, where the shades of the dead go, had set out to entangle the psalmist. Behind this lies the identification in Hebrew thought of "the deep," the chaotic elements out of which the universe came at the creative word (Gen. 1:2), and of Sheol, the place of shadowy existence and meaninglessness where the dead dwelt.

The wrath of the Lord is manifested in an upheaval of nature in the midst of which he shows his glory. The general setting for this description (vss. 8-16) seems to be a thunderstorm with its thunder, lightning, and black clouds. The thunder is the sound of the Lord's mighty voice. The lightning is the blazing forth of his glorious presence as he rides on the wings of the wind and covers himself with the cloud canopy; it can also be described as his arrows. The sense that God discloses himself in blazing light at the same time that he hides himself in clouds and thick darkness is a reminder that the Lord remains mysterious even as he reveals himself. The storm sweeps over the sea and lays bare its channels and the foundations of the world. This phrase is understandable when we remember the primitive cosmology of the time. The earth was thought of as a flat disc floating in the all-embracing and chaotic deep. This deep was also piled up above the heavenly firmament which rested on its mountain pillars or foundations at the earth's edge. God reached down and delivered his suppliant, bringing him into a broad place.

Verses 21-31: The theme now changes from deliverance to reward. For the Hebrews, the emphasis is upon personal righteousness, which in some sense puts a claim on God. There is not the New Testament emphasis on moral righteousness as the work of God's Spirit in a man's life. "Righteousness" is essentially a legal term, as we have seen, meaning conformance to the required norm of conduct—God's statutes and ordinances. God fixes this norm or standard. He is righteous in himself, and this standard is the expression of his own character and he abides true to himself.

Verses 32-46: Once more the theme changes and God is now praised as the One who empowers his servant. Strength, cunning, and skill in war are his gifts. He makes victory possible over Israel's enemies, and the psalmist celebrates triumph in war in savage terms hardly consonant with the spirit of the New Testament. Once more we have to remember the time in which the words were written. At least the emphasis falls on reliance on God, who exalts his servant so that aliens may turn to him.

Verses 47-51: The psalm closes with a cry of blessing and thanksgiving, a doxology of praise. The Lord is the living God, an expression that embraces the thought of God as an active, dynamic presence, intervening in the affairs of his people and acting in history. He is the rock of salvation, a recurring thought which emphasizes the security that he gives. The last verse celebrates once more God's steadfast covenant love toward David and his house.

David's Testament (23:1-7)

This psalm is very confused in its text and the meaning is not always clear. It is probable that, in its original form, it goes back to David. As it is, it presents an idealized picture of him compared with the one in the contemporary records that we have been discussing. The skillful warrior and shrewd ruler, with his sins and failings, is replaced by a religious hero who, as God's anointed, is marked by deep piety. David is pictured as a just ruler, under whom Israel enjoys prosperity (vss. 3-4). The everlasting Covenant of the Lord with David's house is celebrated (vs. 5), and the doom of the evil and godless is seen in the declaration that they will go down before the weapons of the righteous (vss. 6-7).

More Mighty Warriors (23:8-39)

We have here a second list of David's heroes, but included in it is a charming story going back to the king's early days as a refugee in the stronghold of Adullam. David craved spring water from the well of Bethlehem, a city occupied by the Philistines. Three of his heroes broke through the Philistine camp and secured the water. David, moved by their faithfulness and love, poured out the precious water on the ground as a sacrifice to the Lord, for it had become as blood in his eyes because of the risk his warriors had taken. We need to remember that, for the Hebrew, the blood contained the life essence and must thus always be poured out to God and never consumed. First Chronicles 11:10-41 has the same list of heroes and offers a better text.

Census and Its Consequences (24:1-25)

This passage gives us an insight into the nature of early Hebrew religion and also into the early history of the Temple site at Jerusalem. The Lord is described as angry with Israel, for no stated reason. Since in those days all events, good and evil, were traced back to the divine will and little account was taken of secondary causes, all calamity was ascribed directly to the divine wrath. Natural causes and human intentions were discounted in comparison with the all-prevailing activity of God himself. There is a deep truth in this, for ultimately all the universe is within God's providential care. Yet the revelation of the Cross means that God grants a degree of freedom to his creation, the consequences of which are borne by him in suffering and redeeming love. That his wrath is operative, none would deny, but it is not irrational as this passage seems to suggest; and always, as we have said earlier, it is motivated by, and is indeed the underside of, his redeeming love. This passage must thus be read with caution, for it seems to suggest that God was irrationally angry with his people and sought an excuse to punish them. He is described as inciting David to take a census. The Chronicler, rewriting the story later in Jewish history, was so disturbed at this that he replaced the name of the Lord by that of Satan and described Satan as inciting David (I Chron. 21:1).

David proceeded to commit the terrible "sin" of numbering the people. Joab objected to the whole plan but was overruled by the king. When, however, the census had been completed, David's conscience was stricken, and he consulted Gad, his prophet. Why taking a census was sinful is by no means clear; probably this was a relic of superstition, although there are suggestions that it betokened pride in military strength and that it might signify reliance on that power rather than on the Lord. Gad came to David with an oracle from the Lord, offering the king three alternatives—seven years of famine, three months of devastation and war, or three days of plague, and David chose the last, preferring to fall into the hands of God through plague rather than into the hands of men in war.

The account personifies the plague as the "angel" of death. The ravages of the plague were so terrible that the divine wrath was satisfied, and God intervened at the point where the pestilence was about to reach into Jerusalem. David's penitence at the threshing floor of Araunah the Jebusite marked the end of the plague. He was instructed by the prophet Gad to secure this site and consecrate it to the worship of the Lord. Araunah met the request to purchase by freely offering the floor as a gift. David refused, however, on the ground that he would not offer burnt offerings to God which had cost him nothing. This conviction underlies all true sacrifice (and all real piety); it found full expression later in the Book of Psalms. A religion which costs nothing is no true religion at all. The site thus purchased was eventually included in the area of Solomon's Temple.